KU-130-282

*Making Sense of*
*English in*
# Psychology

Jenny Roberts

# Chambers

Published 1993 by Chambers Harrap Publishers Ltd
43–45 Annandale Street, Edinburgh EH7 4AZ

© Jenny Roberts 1993

All rights reserved. No part of this publication may be
reproduced, stored in a retrieval system, or transmitted,
in any form or by any means, electronic, mechanical,
photocopying, recording or otherwise, without the prior
permission of Chambers Harrap Publishers Ltd.

A catalogue record for this book is available from the
British Library

ISBN 0 550 18048 6

Typeset by Hewer Text Composition Services, Edinburgh
Printed in England by Clays Ltd, St Ives plc

*Making Sense of*
*English in*

# Psychology

*Other titles in the series:*

Making Sense of English Usage
Making Sense of Foreign Words in English
Making Sense of English in Money Matters
Making Sense of English in the Law
Making Sense of English in Religion
Making Sense of English in Alternative Medicine
Making Sense of English in Computers
Making Sense of English in Sex

# Contents

Preface                                    vi

Pronunciation Guide                        viii

**Psychology**                             1

# Preface

Psychology is a notoriously difficult term to define. The word literally means 'science of the mind', but most dictionaries would extend this to include the concept of 'behaviour' and offer a brief definition such as 'the study or science of human and animal mind and behaviour'.

The minds and behaviour of ourselves and others are of absorbing interest to most of us, and people with no professional interest or training in the subject are fascinated by psychology. However, there is considerable confusion among many lay people as to terminology, and particularly regarding the distinctions between psychology, psychiatry, psychotherapy, psychoanalysis, and so on. When I used to tell people that I was studying psychology I was amused at the number who responded by muttering darkly that I'd be able to know everything that they were thinking. And in a recent television documentary a woman was heard to say that her idea of psychiatry was 'lying on a couch looking at inkblots'. It is true that most psychoanalysts do actually use a couch for their patients, and that some psychiatrists and clinical psychologists make use of inkblot tests as a diagnostic device, but the two are unlikely to be encountered in juxtaposition! The popular conception of psychology and its related disciplines is often fed by ill-informed stereotypes, and it is hoped that this book might sort out some of the confusion and misunderstanding.

This book is not a dictionary of psychology. The broad definition of the subject given above obviously covers an enormously wide range, and the book certainly does not attempt to provide an exhaustive list of all the terminology used in every aspect of psychology. Neither is the book intended for those studying psychology as an academic discipline. It is primarily an attempt to explain some of the most commonly encountered and most interesting terms, and how these terms are used by professionals. It is aimed at lay people who have an interest in clarifying what the terms mean and how they are used.

Many of the entries here deal with very basic and central areas in psychology that are important to anyone with an interest in the subject. Others are less central and are included for various reasons. Although psychoanalysis is peripheral to the central areas of psychology, it is undeniable that the theories of Freud, Jung, and Adler have had a very significant impact on our thought and language. Terms such as *ego, libido, defence mechanism, inferiority complex,* or *introvert* are in common use; these and other such terms are explained here within the context of their originators' basic theories.

Some terms are included because they may impinge on the readers' lives or those of their families or friends. If your son is diagnosed as *hyperactive* or your daughter is said to have a high *IQ*; if your father has *senile dementia* or your mother is prescribed *electroconvulsive therapy*; if your best friend is *manic-depressive*; if your boss wants to send you on a course for *sensitivity training*, then it is important that you know what these terms imply, and how the professionals you may encounter use them. Other terms are included because they are connected with much-discussed topics (for example, *post-traumatic stress disorder*); others, particularly terms from social psychology, are intrinsically interesting because of what they reveal about human motivation and behaviour.

Some of the terms included are unlikely to be found in conventional textbooks of psychology. This is sometimes because they are terms that are not, or are no longer, used by professionals although they remain popular with lay people (eg *nervous breakdown* or *mass hysteria*); sometimes it is because they are not technical terms at all but nevertheless are terms frequently used by therapists and counsellors.

There is very little included on animal behaviour, or on the more technical aspects of physiological psychology and such fields as the psychology of perception,

Finally, although the book is concerned with 'making sense of English', in fact many of the words used in psychology are actually Latin or Greek words, some are German or French, and many more are translated or derived from foreign languages. Where the linguistic background of a term is interesting, or helps to explain its meaning, the entry includes a brief discussion of its origin.

Jenny Roberts

# Pronunciation Guide

**Vowels**

| | | |
|---|---|---|
| iː | need | /niːd/ |
| ɪ | pit | /pɪt/ |
| i | very | /ˈvɛri/ |
| ɛ | pet | /pɛt/ |
| æ | pat | /pæt/ |
| ʌ | other | /ˈʌðəʳ/ |
| ʊ | book | /bʊk/ |
| uː | too | /tuː/ |
| u | influence | /ˈɪnfluəns/ |
| ɒ | cough | /kɒf/ |
| ɔː | ought | /ɔːt/ |
| ɜː | work | /wɜːk/ |
| ə | another | /əˈnʌðəʳ/ |
| ɑː | part | /pɑːt/ |

**Glides**

| | | |
|---|---|---|
| eɪ | plate | /pleɪt/ |
| aɪ | sigh | /saɪ/ |
| ɔɪ | ploy | /plɔɪ/ |
| oʊ | go | /goʊ/ |
| aʊ | now | /naʊ/ |
| ɪə | hear | /hɪəʳ/ |
| ɛə | fair | /fɛəʳ/ |
| ʊə | poor | /pʊəʳ/ |

**Consonants**

| | | |
|---|---|---|
| p | pit | /pɪt/ |
| b | bit | /bɪt/ |
| t | ten | /tɛn/ |
| d | den | /dɛn/ |
| k | cap | /kæp/ |
| g | gap | /gæp/ |
| ʃ | shin | /ʃɪn/ |
| ʒ | pleasure | /ˈplɛʒəʳ/ |
| ʧ | chin | /ʧɪn/ |
| ʤ | budge | /bʌʤ/ |
| h | hit | /hɪt/ |
| f | fit | /fɪt/ |
| v | very | /ˈvɛri/ |
| θ | thin | /θɪn/ |
| ð | then | /ðɛn/ |
| s | sin | /sɪn/ |
| z | zones | /zoʊnz/ |
| m | meat | /miːt/ |
| n | knit | /nɪt/ |
| ŋ | sing | /sɪŋ/ |
| l | line | /laɪn/ |
| r | rid | /rɪd/ |
| j | yet | /jɛt/ |
| w | quick | /kwɪk/ |

**Other symbols**

ʳ   indicates an 'r' pronounced only before a following vowel

ˈ   precedes the syllable with primary stress

**Note**

Words or phrases within an entry that are printed in **bold type** refer the reader to another entry where there is further relevant information. *Italic type* is used within entries to indicate significant related words that do not themselves have an entry (although they may have a cross-reference). Sources of words are also shown in italic type.

# A

### ability

The degree of power, competence, or proficiency that is present to enable an individual to perform a particular mental or physical act. It must be distinguished from **aptitude**; to say that someone has the ability to do something means that the person is able to perform the thing now, with no further training. Many of the tests used in **educational psychology**, such as **intelligence tests**, are tests of ability.

### abnormal psychology

The branch of psychology that deals with behaviour that is considered to diverge from the norm. Because there is so much disagreement about what constitutes abnormality, the term is disliked by some psychologists. The term *psychopathology* is sometimes preferred, but this does not imply any particular study of the **psychopathic personality**; abnormal psychology deals with all kinds of psychological disturbances.

### abreaction

The mental process by which patients experience release of emotional tension by 'reliving' an **anxiety**-arousing situation from their past which they had previously repressed. The situation may be real or imagined, and the reliving can be through words or actions. It can happen spontaneously, but is more usually provoked during therapy, sometimes by **hypnosis**. Abreaction is usually a feature of **psychotherapy** and **psychoanalysis**, but it has sometimes been used by **psychiatrists** in conjunction with injectable barbiturate drugs which repress inhibitions and facilitate recall of suppressed memories. It is also known as *catharsis*.

### accommodation

An adaptation or adjustment made in order to deal with a particular situation. It is a very general term, but is used specifically in psychology in two quite different ways. In **social psychology** it is used to mean the kind of compromise or agreement that people enter into so as to maintain social harmony within a group or between two or more opposing groups. In **Piagetian theory** it means the way children modify their existing intellectual structures when new experiences cannot be assimilated by them.

See also **assimilation**

## achievement need

See **need for achievement**

## acquired drive

Any **drive** whose motivating forces have been learned or acquired, rather than arising from physiological needs; sometimes known as *secondary drive*. A simple example of an acquired drive is **fear**; at a more sophisticated level, the desire for money is often given as an example.

See also **primary drive**

## acrophobia

An abnormal, irrational fear of heights. As with all phobic conditions, the irrationality must be stressed. The anxiety experienced by most people when, for example, they are standing on the top of an unstable ladder, is not acrophobia, as there is a very real danger of falling. It is derived from the Greek word *acro* 'topmost' or 'extremity', together with **phobia**.

## acting out

A term sometimes used in a general way to refer to any uncontrollable outburst of irrational behaviour. In **psychoanalysis** it is used for the behaviour of a patient — often one with **behaviour disorders** or a **psychopathic personality** – who has a strong impulse to engage in some kind of overt behaviour and is unable to express the impulse verbally, or to reflect on the origin or meaning of the activity. It is thought that the behaviour, which is often aggressive in nature, is a substitute for remembering significant events in the patient's past, and therefore a patient who is acting out is often not able to respond to psychoanalysis.

## adaptation

A term used generally in psychology to refer to responses made to changes in the environment. In **experimental psychology** it is used to describe a reaction to an applied stimulus (eg *dark* *adaptation* is used for the way the eye adjusts to reduced illumination). In **social psychology**, adaptation is used to describe the way people's behaviour changes in order to satisfy either the changing expectations of the society they are in, or the new demands of a different environment. In **psychoanalysis** the emphasis is on the individual being able to act effectively on the environment by discriminating between inner **fantasy** and external perception.

## Adlerian /æd'lɪərɪən/ *or* /ɑ:d'lɪərɪən/
A term referring to the theories of the Austrian psychiatrist Alfred Adler (1870–1937), or to those whose psychotherapeutic practice demonstrates these theories. Adler was an early disciple of Freud, but broke away from him to form his own movement. His theories, sometimes known as **individual psychology**, are based on the idea that the most important human drive is the desire for power, and that people are constantly struggling to overcome, and compensate for, **conscious** or **unconscious** feelings of inferiority.
See also **compensation; guiding fiction; inferiority complex**

## affect
A term used in psychology to refer to feelings and emotions, and used more or less synonymously with *emotion, feeling*, and *mood*. The word can only be used as a noun in this psychological sense, and should not be confused with the noun *effect*. It is pronounced with the stress on the first syllable.
See also **emotion; inappropriate affect**

## affective disorder
A diagnostic term used in **psychiatry** to embrace a number of different disorders which are all characterized by disturbances of the **affect**, ie the mood or emotions. Usually this involves the expression of excessive depression or elation. **Manic depression** and **depression** are both classed as affective disorders.

## aggression
A term used very generally in psychology to refer to hostile or destructive behaviour or **attitudes**, but also used in more specialized ways in a number of different contexts, and in a variety of ways according to the particular theory held by the

user. It is often used in conjunction with another term, such as *territorial aggression* (aggression used to defend one's own territory) or *instrumental aggression* (aggression used merely as a means to an end). In **social-learning theory**, aggressive behaviour is regarded as a response learned through imitation and subsequent **reinforcement**. In **Freudian** theory, aggression is thought of as a manifestation of the **death instinct**, whereas **Adlerian** theorists see it as being linked to the desire for power. Some regard it as a **primary drive**; others as a reaction to frustration.

## agoraphobia

A **phobia** about open spaces. It derives from Greek *agora* 'public meeting-place, market-place', and in fact sufferers frequently experience **anxiety** about public places and crowds, as well as open spaces. In some cases, fear of leaving the security of the home and facing a possible panic attack outside can be so severe that agoraphobics can become virtually housebound. Although agoraphobia is popularly thought of as the opposite of **claustrophobia**, it is not uncommon for people to suffer from both.

## aim-inhibition

In **psychoanalysis**, interpersonal relationships where the **unconscious** motive lying behind the relationship is inhibited. As **Freudian** theory places such an emphasis on unconscious sexual **motivation**, aim-inhibition usually refers to non-sexual friendships and family relationships, where it is assumed that there is **inhibition** of an unconscious erotic interest in the object.

## alienation

A term used with various nuances of meaning in different branches of psychology, but always with the suggestion of the individual's feelings of estrangement, powerlessness, strangeness, and separation from other people. In **existential psychology**, there is also the sense of alienation from oneself, the strangeness that people feel when their actions, dictated by outside pressures towards conformity, do not seem to relate to what they see as their inner or 'real' self. Alienation was formerly also a word for **insanity**, and psychiatrists were known as *alienists*. This use persists in the USA, where an alienist is an expert on legal aspects of insanity.

## Alzheimer's disease /'æltshaɪməz/

A progressive form of **dementia**, in which the familiar symptoms of senility — memory loss, speech and personality disturbances – are displayed, but which can strike as early as the 40s and 50s. It is caused by degeneration of nerve cells in the brain, and there is at present no effective treatment. It is named after a German physician, Alois Alzheimer (1887–1967), and is also known as *presenile dementia*.

## ambiguity, tolerance of

See **tolerance of ambiguity**

## ambivalence

A term used in psychology in a similar way to ordinary English usage, to mean contradictory **attitudes** and feelings towards the same object. It is sometimes used for cases where the contrasting feelings exist simultaneously, and sometimes for cases where a person frequently oscillates between the two feelings. In **psychoanalysis**, it almost always refers to love-hate emotions towards a person. In psychological studies of conflict, ambivalence is used in connection with the idea of being drawn towards two different and opposing goals.

See also **approach-approach conflict; approach-avoidance conflict; avoidance-avoidance conflict**

## amnesia

A term generally used to indicate partial or complete loss of memory; from Greek, 'forgetfulness'. Amnesia sometimes has physiological causes, usually brain damage from illness, accident, or alcohol abuse; sometimes it has psychological causes. If it is caused by a physical or psychological **trauma** it is known as *post-traumatic amnesia*. Memory loss for events following the causative trauma is known as *anterograde amnesia*, while *retrograde amnesia* is used for cases when the patient cannot remember events prior to the causative trauma.

See also **infantile amnesia**

## anal character

In **psychoanalysis**, an adult with characteristics appearing to result from being fixated at the **anal stage** of development. The *anal retentive* character is marked by extreme tidiness, orderliness, punctuality, meticulous attention to detail, obstinacy, parsimony, and a tendency to hoard or make collections. Less common is the *anal expulsive* character, who is pliant, untidy, and generous.

## anal stage

An aspect of **psychoanalytic** theory which has given rise to the popular view that psychoanalysts believe all personality defects result from early toilet training. It refers to the stage of infantile development when the child is preoccupied with the functions of the anus. This stage is thought to be important both in the development of the **libido** and the **ego**. Infants derive sensuous pleasure from the process of defecating, but also develop early **socialization** of impulses as they learn to control the anal sphincter. Excessive frustration at this stage (eg through harsh toilet training) can result in the child growing up to display an **anal character**.

## analysand

Someone undergoing **psychoanalysis**. The word was apparently coined because students who were undergoing analysis as part of their training to become **psychoanalysts** objected to being referred to as 'patients'. In fact most analysts and analytic **psychotherapists** normally refer to their patients as 'patients' or 'clients'.

## analysis

See **psychoanalysis**

## analyst

See **psychoanalyst**

## analytic psychology

See **Jungian**

## analytic psychotherapist

See **psychoanalyst**

## angst /æŋst/

A term much used in **existential psychology** to express the

mental anguish of those who realize that the human condition is one where essential personal choices must be made in a meaningless world: from German, 'worry, anxiety, fear'. In **psychoanalysis** it is used more or less synonymously with **anxiety**.
See also **fear**

## anima /ˈænɪmə/

A term used in two different ways in **Jungian** psychology; from Latin, 'soul'. In Jung's earlier writings he used it to mean a person's true inner self, the **psyche** that was in touch with the **unconscious**. Later, Jung developed the idea that both essentially female and essentially male elements were present in both men and women. He then used the term anima to refer to the feminine **archetype** which is present in the male unconscious. This latter sense is usually intended when the word is used now.
See also **animus**

## animus /ˈænɪməs/

A Latin word with various different meanings, including 'spirit' and 'anger'. It is used generally in psychology to mean an intense and long-lasting dislike. It is also used in **Jungian** psychology for the masculine **archetype** that is found in the female **unconscious**.
See also **anima**

## Anna O

An early and famous case history in **psychoanalysis**. 'Anna O' (actually Bertha Pappenheim) was a patient treated by Freud's colleague, the Viennese physician Josef Breuer (1842–1925). She had a variety of physical symptoms, including a paralysis of her arm. When she talked to Breuer under **hypnosis** and recalled that the paralysis had begun when she had fallen asleep at her father's death-bed, her symptoms disappeared. On the basis of this case, Freud developed the theory that repressed memories can cause hysterical symptoms, and that their cure lies in psychoanalysis.
See also **conversion hysteria**

## anomie /ˈænəmi/

A term used in two different ways in **social psychology**; from Greek, 'lawlessness'. It can refer to a situation of social instability, where there is confusion and a breakdown of social structure and values. This might happen after a war or a major natural disaster. Anomie is also used for the **alienation**, loss of identity, and feelings of isolation experienced by individuals in well-organized and highly developed societies. It can also be spelled **anomy**, and some writers use *anomie* for the first sense described above and *anomy* for the second.

**anorexia nervosa** /ænə'rɛksiə nɜ:'voʊsə/
One of the most common **eating disorders**. *Anorexia* comes from Greek and means 'loss of appetite', while *nervosa* suggests the 'nervous' or psychological origin of the condition. It is characterized by an obsessive fear of becoming overweight, an aversion to eating, and severe weight loss. The typical sufferer is a young woman, often from a middle- or upper-class background. Patients usually have an extremely distorted **body image**, seeing themselves as grossly fat, when in fact they are becoming emaciated. Both physiological and psychiatric treatment are necessary; if treatment is not successful the condition can result in death.
See also **bulimia**

**antisocial personality**
A fairly recent term, used for those with a history of antisocial behaviour, starting in childhood and continuing into adult life. Such behaviour may include lying, theft, sexual and other forms of aggression, or drug and alcohol abuse, and is always marked by a disregard for the rights of others in the society. The antisocial personality is similar to the **psychopathic personality**, but the lack of guilt associated with the latter is not such a significant characteristic.

**anxiety**
A word used with various shades of meaning in psychology. The usual meaning of an unpleasant emotional state characterized by uneasy feelings of apprehension and dread is present in psychological usage, but to be considered as a symptom, the state must be abnormally severe. It is sometimes accompanied by physical manifestations such as sweating and palpitations and, unlike **fear**, it is often without any object. In **psychoanalytic** theory, the emphasis is on mental conflict rather than

physical symptoms. According to Freud, there are two kinds of anxiety: *signal anxiety* is a mechanism by which the **ego** is in a state of tension and is forewarned to construct some **defence mechanism** to protect it from *primary anxiety*, which produces nightmares and the sort of symptoms discussed above. In **existential psychology** anxiety is equivalent to **angst**.

One other specialized use of anxiety occurs within a theory of how learning takes place. Anxiety is regarded as an **acquired drive** which motivates an avoidance response, ie a mental or physical movement away from a goal. The avoidance response is reinforced by a reduction in anxiety.

See also **free-floating anxiety; separation anxiety; test anxiety**

## aphasia /əˈfeɪzɪə/ *or* /əˈfeɪʒə/
Partial or total loss of the ability to use or understand speech; from Greek *phasis* 'speech, utterance'; less commonly known as *dysphasia*. Aphasia is not applied to conditions whose origins are wholly psychological, but only to those arising from some kind of brain damage.

## applied psychology
A general term for all branches of psychology which apply psychological theories to practical areas, including sub-disciplines such as **educational psychology** and **industrial psychology**. Applied psychology also encompasses the use of **psychologists** in areas such as design, market research, criminal investigations, or the handling of sieges, riots, and hostage taking. It further includes the study of basic principles of psychology with the aim of applying them in practical aspects of everyday life.

## approach-approach conflict
A conflict caused by having to choose between two goals that are equally desirable but incompatible with each other. A trivial example might be the conflict between getting up and making coffee or having some more sleep; a more serious one might be choosing whether to spend three years in higher education or to get a job and earn money. As goals are thought to become more desirable the closer one is to them, the conflict is usually resolved by moving closer to one of the goals, thus making that the more desirable of the two.

## approach-avoidance conflict

A conflict caused by being both attracted towards and repelled by the same goal, for example someone might need to cross the Atlantic as quickly as possible but have a fear of flying. It is usually resolved by adjusting one of the conflicting feelings towards the goal, so that the other dominates.

## aptitude

The potential for achievement or for acquiring a particular skill after training. Tests of aptitude are widely used in **educational psychology** and other areas. Some of them are very general, and vary little from tests of **ability**. However, the intention is not just to measure the subject's power to perform at the moment, but to make predictions as to what the person might be capable of. Other aptitude tests are much more specific, and designed to ascertain, for example, whether a child has musical or scientific aptitude, or whether a person has the potential for training as, say, a pilot or a computer programmer.

## archetype /ɑ:kɪtaɪp/

A term in **Jungian** psychological theory; it derives from Greek *archetypos* 'original pattern or model', and is closely related to Jung's central theory of the **collective unconscious**. The archetypes are part of our inherited innate unconscious ideas and present themselves to us as images and symbols. These include religious and geometric symbols and the material of myth and fairytales, such as giants or unicorns. They also present themselves in dreams, particularly when a person is in a state of heightened emotion.

## art therapy

The use of art in a therapeutic setting, usually involving patients in drawing, painting, or modelling, in order to express their emotional state and achieve release from tension. It is not normally used in isolation, but as just one part of the rehabilitation or treatment of a patient.

## assertiveness training

A variety of techniques designed to help people to assert their opinions and needs. Originally it was used as therapy for patients with **social phobias** and other disorders whose symptoms included timidity, passivity, and lack of confidence. However, it has become a very popular form of training programme for all who experience difficulty in boldly expressing their own emotions, views, and desires. Training is normally in groups and involves discussion and **role play**. Although in ordinary English *assertiveness* is often more or less synonymous with *aggressiveness*, it is important in assertiveness training to learn to avoid aggressive behaviour and **attitudes** as well as timid ones.

## assimilation

A term with a great many meanings in different branches of psychology, all of them having some connotation of 'taking in' or 'incorporating'. In **Piagetian theory** it is used to mean the way children apply their established intellectual **schema** to new experiences in their environment. It is also used in theories of learning to describe the way novel ideas or events have to be incorporated into the existing cognitive structure in order to become memorizable. It can be used as an opposite term to **repression** for the incorporation of unpleasant facts etc into the individual's experience, and Jung uses it for the way individuals change events or ideas so as to fit in with their emotional needs. *Cultural* or *social assimilation* is used in **social psychology** for the process whereby individuals or groups with different ethnic or cultural backgrounds merge into the dominant culture of the society in which they live.

## association

A very general term for the learned connection between two ideas, events, images, etc. The concept dates back to Aristotle and is the basis for various psychological theories about memory, learning, and cognitive processes.
See also **free association**

## attachment

A very close, usually interdependent, emotional bond between people. It is used particularly to describe the relationship that develops between an infant and the adult or adults that it is closest to, so that the infant appears to feel safe in their company and becomes anxious when separated from them.
See also **bonding; separation anxiety**

## attention-deficit disorder

A syndrome found in children and characterized by failure to concentrate or attend for more than a very short space of time, hyperactive behaviour, aggression, and a marked impulsiveness; also known as **hyperkinesis** and **hyperactive child syndrome**. It can be caused by slight brain dysfunction or have emotional origins.

See also **hyperactivity**

## attitudes

A word derived from the same root as **aptitude**, and originally meaning 'fitness', in the sense of being fit to perform a task. However, its meaning has moved away from the idea of 'potential' and come to represent the predisposition to react in a certain way to ideas, people, situations, etc. In theories of **personality** and **social psychology**, attitudes are recognized as having several elements: affective factors involving the emotions; evaluative factors involving judgement and appraisal; cognitive factors involving beliefs; and 'conative' factors involving the disposition for action.

## attitude testing

The use of devices designed to reveal people's **attitudes** and measure their strength. The devices are usually in the form of paper and pencil tests where the subject is given a series of statements representing attitudes and asked to mark a point on a scale according to whether they 'agree strongly', 'agree slightly', etc down to 'disagree strongly'. They are used most often in **social psychology** and in areas of **applied psychology** such as market research and opinion polling.

See also **Likert scale**

## attribution

The process of ascribing characteristics, **motivation**, etc to ourselves and other people. This is done by observing someone's behaviour, and attributing fundamental motivational characteristics to the person which appear to be consistent with his or her overt behaviour. There are various theories of attribution in **social psychology**, but in non-technical terms, attribution might be said to be the basic process of trying to understand 'what makes people tick', which is central to psychology and to ordinary life

## authoritarian personality

A person who is characterized by the following traits: a belief in strict obedience and submission to authority, conventionalism, respect for power and toughness combined with contempt for weakness, low **tolerance of ambiguity**, rigidity, superstition, incapacity for self-blame, and lack of self-insight. This cluster of personality traits was defined by American **psychologists** in the 1940s and 1950s, as a result of testing subjects with a specially designed attitude scale (see **attitude testing**), as well as a series of structured interviews and **projective techniques**. The attitude scale was designed to establish a link between the authoritarian personality and **ethnocentrism**, antisemitism, and antidemocratic attitudes. It is interesting to note that although the authoritarian personality is characterized by a strong belief in obedience to authority, when psychologists tested prisoners in the notorious San Quentin jail in California, they found that a majority of them demonstrated authoritarian personality traits.

## autism

A condition characterized by absorption in self-centred mental activity and withdrawal from reality; the word literally means 'self-orientation'. Although *autism* and *autistic* can be applied to anyone exhibiting these characteristics, the word is almost always used to mean the severe pathological condition that first appears in childhood.

An autistic person is typically unresponsive to other people, lacks **empathy** and imagination, is unable to form friendships or attachments, is extremely withdrawn, and has difficulties with language and communication. Some autistic people compulsively repeat stereotyped movements or bizarre actions for hours on end. It is not uncommon for autistic people to develop an interest in some particular activity and exhibit an extraordinary ability to concentrate on it. There are various theories as to the causes of autism: some believe it arises from brain damage; others think that it is a form of **schizophrenia**. There is no cure, but autistic people can improve their communication skills and responsiveness if treated in a very structured and predictable environment.

## autosuggestion

Techniques of influencing one's behaviour, ways of thought, or physical health by suggestions coming from one's own mind; the term literally means 'self-suggestion'. It was invented by Emile Coué (1857–1926), a French pharmacist and student of **hypnosis**, who claimed to have helped people to effect improvements in their mental and physical condition by teaching them the repetition of the phrase 'Every day, and in every way, I am becoming better and better'.

## aversion therapy

A form of **behaviour modification**, using techniques of **conditioning** and designed to change undesirable behaviour by associating it with unpleasant stimuli. The aversive stimuli used are generally electric shocks or drugs. Alcoholics are sometimes treated by aversion therapy by giving them a drug which, when combined with alcohol, produces nausea. Aversion therapy has also been used with supposed sexual deviants, who are shown pictures of the desired sexual object while a slight electric shock is administered.

## avoidance-avoidance conflict

A conflict caused by having to choose between two goals which are equally unattractive, for example staying in an unpleasant job or being unemployed. It is usually resolved by deciding that one of the goals is the 'lesser evil' and choosing that.

# B

## balance theory

A theory associated with the American psychologist Fritz Heider (1896– ). It is based on the view that people seek to avoid the tension caused by their beliefs being in a state of imbalance. If, for example, one encounters an experience that is incompatible with one's existing beliefs, one would have to explain the experience away to oneself so as to restore balance. Balance theory is used as a collective term to embrace all psychological theories that are based on the human need for equilibrium in **attitudes**, including **cognitive dissonance**.

## basic trust/mistrust

Important concepts in the developmental theories of the German-born **psychoanalyst** Erik Erikson (1902– ). Basic mistrust is established immediately at birth by the **birth trauma**, but if infants are cared for by a loving, confident, and reliable person during their first 18 months, they develop a sense of security and basic trust in themselves and their environment. If they do not experience this sort of caring, infants will continue in a state of basic mistrust of themselves and their environment, suspicion of others, and **anxiety**.

## battle fatigue

See **combat fatigue**

## behaviour disorders

A diagnostic term in **psychiatry**, used to cover all conditions characterized by aberrant and unacceptable behaviour that is severe enough to need treatment. In children and adolescents, such behaviour might include **aggression**, self-destructive behaviour, truancy, and stealing.

## behaviourism

A school of psychology founded by the American psychologist J B Watson (1878–1958). Its basic theory is that psychology can study only objective observable behaviour, and that the introspective study of feelings, emotions, etc is impossible to verify and is therefore of no interest to psychology. Early behaviourism has been superseded by rather more subtle theories, including **Skinnerian** theories, but behaviourism still remains a dominant influence in psychology, particularly in the USA.

## behaviour modification

The application of **conditioning** techniques to the treatment of psychological disorders and problems. It is usually used synonymously with *behaviour therapy*, and is based on theories marked by a lack of interest in any underlying causes of problem behaviour. Behaviour modification focuses on the overt behaviour presented, and assumes that, as all behaviour is learned, people can be helped to change their behaviour by relearning and reconditioning techniques. It is used mainly to treat **behaviour disorders** and **phobias**.

See also **aversion therapy; behaviourism; cognitive behaviour modification; desensitization; token economy**

## behaviour therapy

See **behaviour modification**

## Binet Scale /'biːneɪ/

The first example of an **intelligence test**, invented by the French psychologist Alfred Binet (1857–1911) in order to predict children's performance on academic tasks at school. The scale was first issued in 1905, then revised in 1908 and 1911. The test items become progressively more difficult, and are standardized by age. Also known as the **Binet-Simon Scale** to include the name of Binet's colleague, Théodore Simon /simɔ̃/.

See also **Stanford-Binet Scale**

## biological psychology

See **physiological psychology**

## bipolar disorder

See **manic depression**

## birth trauma

The theory that all **anxiety** arises from the original **trauma** of being born. This universal experience of being thrust from the comfort and security of the womb produces an anxiety which is reactivated by weaning and all further experiences of separation from the mother and other loved people and objects. The theory was formulated by the Austrian psychoanalyst Otto Rank (1884–1939), an early follower of Freud.

## body image

The picture that a person has of what his or her body looks like, especially how it appears to other people. The image often fails to catch up with actual bodily changes caused by aging etc, but this is not abnormal. However, a very distorted or inaccurate body image, as in **anorexia nervosa**, is a symptom of disorder.

## body language

Non-verbal communication between people, conveying information about emotions and **attitudes** through **conscious** or **unconscious** facial expression, gestures, and posture. It has become popular in the training of counsellors, who are often guided as to which features of body language convey approachability, appear threatening, etc and in therapies such as **assertiveness training**.

## bonding

The forming of a close emotional link between people. It is used especially of the bond between a new-born infant and its mother: sometimes synonymously with **attachment** to describe the more long-term relationship, and sometimes to describe the immediate forming of an emotional link in the hours or days following birth.

## boomerang effect

In **social psychology**, a change in someone's **attitude** in the opposite direction from the change being advocated. For example, someone who had had a neutral attitude towards a religion may become fiercely opposed to it as a result of insensitive proselytizing.

## borderline

An adjective used in various ways in psychology, but always with the implication that cases lie near the dividing line between different categories. When applied to **intelligence** or **mental retardation**, borderline suggests cases at the boundary between being able to live a normal life and needing institutional help. An **IQ** range of 70–80 is often cited. Borderline was previously used diagnostically in **abnormal psychology** to characterize those whose disorders seemed to lie between **neurosis** and **psychosis**. However, as these concepts are now used less frequently, borderline is more often applied to specific disorders (eg *borderline personality disorder, borderline schizophrenia*), for those whose symptoms do not quite fit the usual description of the disorder.

## boundaries

A non-technical term often used by psychotherapists and counsellors in the dictionary sense of 'something that fixes a limit'. The particular application is usually to the limits fixed to a person's behaviour, and probably set by other people. It is often applied to children, in terms of the boundaries, explicit or implicit, set by their parents and guiding them as to what behaviour is acceptable and what unacceptable. It may also be used in relation to the limits that people establish for themselves in compartmentalizing aspects of their lives, eg 'creating clear boundaries between work and personal life'.

## brainstorming

A problem-solving technique originating in the USA, and used in **social psychology**, **industrial psychology**, and other areas of **applied psychology**. It involves a group of people all participating in the quickfire generation of ideas for the solution of a particular problem.

## brainwashing

A systematic attempt to change someone's ideas, **attitudes**, or behaviour through the application of various kinds of emotional or physical pressure; also sometimes known as *coercive persuasion*. It is usually applied to the attempt to manipulate people into abandoning their former beliefs and loyalties and accepting a different ideology. The word is a translation of a Chinese term, as the technique came to be known through the experiences of prisoners of war in China under the Communist regime.

## breakthrough

In **psychotherapy**, a sudden advance in a patient's treatment, usually after a long period where no progress was being made. It often describes a patient's overcoming resistance to thinking about a particular difficulty and suddenly gaining an insight into its causes etc.

## bulimia /bjuˈlɪmɪə/

Originally an abnormal and constant craving for food, from Greek *bous* 'ox, head of cattle' + *limos* 'hunger'. It is now used of an **eating disorder** in which the patient goes on binges, eating enormous quantities of food, and then vomits, either naturally or by self-induced means. These episodes are usually accompanied by guilt and **depression**. As with **anorexia nervosa**, *bulimic* patients are often very much concerned with their weight and with dieting, and in fact it is not uncommon for patients to alternate between periods of anorexia and of bulimia.

## bystander effect

A phenomenon observed by researchers in **social psychology**. It suggests that the greater the number of people present in a situation where help is needed – such as an accident or emergency – the less likely it is for any of them to offer aid. As the number of bystanders increases, people's sense of responsibility diminishes, each person assuming that someone else will help.

# C

### career counselling
See **vocational counselling**

### castration complex
A term in **Freudian** theory. In males it refers to the supposed universal male **anxiety** about losing the genitals, arising from childhood fears that masturbation or sexual **fantasy** may be punished by castration. In females the complex stems from guilt in childhood arising from the belief that this punitive castration has already taken place, as demonstrated by their lack of a penis. **Psychotherapists** now refer to *castration anxiety* for the more general and symbolic threat that men experience with regard to their genitals and masculinity. Advances in understanding of female sexuality have cast considerable doubt on the application of the theory to women.
See also **penis envy**

### catalepsy
A state of muscular rigidity, where the body will remain in one position for long periods of time; from a Greek word meaning 'to seize'. It is seen in various severe psychological disorders and under **hypnosis**. It is not to be confused with *cataplexy*, a sudden loss of muscle tone usually caused by shock.
See also **catatonia**

### cataplexy
See **catalepsy**

### catatonia
A syndrome sometimes found in **schizophrenia**. It is characterized by **catalepsy**, in which the patient is rigid and usually does not speak for weeks or even months at a time, alternating with periods of extreme excitement and activity. It is a hybrid word, formed from Greek *kata* 'down, wrong' + Latin *tonus*, referring to muscular tone or tension.

### catharsis
See **abreaction**

### censorship
In **psychoanalysis**, the **repression** of **unconscious** thoughts, desires, and ideas to prevent them from emerging into the **conscious** state. Freud's early theories of a *censor* developed into the theory of the **superego**.

### certifiable
A term used popularly to mean 'mad enough to warrant psychiatric treatment, whether voluntarily or not'. It is not used in **psychiatry** except as a legal term to apply to a person whom medical experts state to be in need of psychiatric treatment or institutionalization.
See also **insanity; section**

### child psychology
A general umbrella term for any form of psychology which concentrates on the study of human beings from birth to adolescence. The most important areas are within **developmental psychology** and **educational psychology**, but practitioners in many other fields, studying both normal and abnormal psychological development and behaviour, may choose to focus on children. There are also **psychoanalysts** and **psychotherapists** who work exclusively with child clients.
See also **Little Hans**

### children with special needs
See **exceptional children**

### classical conditioning
An experimental procedure, and the learning that takes place through following it; also known as **Pavlovian conditioning**, after the Russian physiologist Ivan Pavlov (1849–1936), on whose research it is based. It involves the repeated pairing of an arbitrary and neutral *conditioned stimulus* with an *unconditioned stimulus* which elicits an **unconditioned response**. In Pavlov's famous experiments, dogs were presented with food (the unconditioned stimulus) at the same time as a bell (the conditioned stimulus) was rung. The unconditioned response

elicited by the food was salivation. Eventually the sound of the bell alone produced the **conditioned response** of salivation.

## classical theory
See **Freudian**

## claustrophobia /klɔːstrəˈfoʊbiə/
An extreme fear of being in narrow and enclosed spaces; from Greek *claustrum* 'confined place' + **phobia**. Sufferers usually experience acute **anxiety** and feelings of suffocation in lifts, phone boxes, underground trains, caves, etc. Some are unable to cope with being in a small room or any room with unopened or curtained windows. Many people with claustrophobia can trace the fear back to a childhood incident of being locked into a cupboard or other confined space.
See also **agoraphobia**

## client-centred therapy
A form of **psychotherapy** in which the therapist takes a completely non-directive and non-judgemental attitude, and accepts what the client says unconditionally. The emphasis is on the therapist's encouragement and clarification of the client's ideas, in order to facilitate the client to solve his or her own problems. The term is usually used specifically with reference to the technique developed and advocated by the American psychologist Carl Rogers (1902–87). A broader term, including similar approaches not associated with Rogers, is *non-directive therapy*.
See also **non-directive counselling**

## clinical psychology
The branch of psychology that deals with the application of psychological methods to the diagnosis and treatment of emotional and behavioural disorders. A clinical **psychologist** is likely to work in one or more of three areas: diagnosis, mainly involving administering various psychological tests and interpreting the results; treatment, practising some form of **psychotherapy**; and research, usually into psychological testing and the efficacy of various treatments. Clinical psychologists differ from **psychiatrists** in not normally having any medical training.

### co-counselling

Counselling of a single client or a group of clients carried out by two, or sometimes more, counsellors working in a team; sometimes called **conjoint counselling** or **team counselling**. Co-counselling is usually conducted with the counsellors working at the same time, but sometimes they work consecutively. The idea is that the different counsellors complement each other by bringing different approaches to the clients' problems, or by being of different sexes.

### coercive persuasion

See **brainwashing**

### cognitive behaviour modification

A form of **psychotherapy**, based on **behaviour modification**, but aimed at altering cognitive processes such as **attitudes**, beliefs, expectations, and self-image. Relearning is effected through **counselling** and psychotherapy, but also through such techniques as self-monitoring and self-evaluation aimed at helping people to understand the beliefs and attitudes that govern their behaviour. It is used in the treatment of individuals with behavioural problems, and sometimes for children with learning problems. There are several more or less synonymous terms: *cognitive behaviour therapy, cognitive restructuring, cognitive modification*. However, the term *cognitive therapy* is properly used for the form of cognitive behaviour modification associated with the American psychologist Aaron Beck (1921– ), which aims at teaching people to conceptualize their experiences in a positive way in order to produce positive feelings and behaviour.

### cognitive development

A very general term used in **cognitive psychology** and **developmental psychology**. It is used to describe the way children's thinking, perception, judgement, and reasoning faculties become increasingly complex as they encounter new experiences and information from their environment, and deal with them primarily through the processes of **accommodation** and **assimilation**.

## cognitive dissonance

In **social psychology**, a type of **balance theory** associated with the American psychologist Leon Festinger (1919–90). Cognitive dissonance is the state of tension that arises when a person holds two inconsistent (dissonant) beliefs, **attitudes**, or ways of thinking (cognitions), or when there is a conflict between a person's belief and behaviour. Examples of such pairs of dissonant cognitions could be: 'I believe the Bible shows us a loving God', 'This Old Testament passage describes an unloving God'; or 'I voluntarily gave up a pleasant weekend at home to attend this course', 'The course is boring and unhelpful'. Because this state is emotionally painful, there is a strong **motivation** to change the situation and reduce the tension. There are various techniques available. One can redescribe one of the cognitive elements so that it is no longer inconsistent with the other, try to avoid dissonant information, seek social support from those in the same state of cognitive dissonance, or change one or both of the attitudes or beliefs.

## cognitive map

A mental representation or pattern formed by experience and expectation of cause-effect and means-ends relationships, and showing how a problem can be solved or a goal achieved. The term was coined by the American psychologist E C Tolman (1886–1959) as a result of his experiments in teaching rats to learn the way through a maze. He came to believe that the rats were not just learning a set of movements, but were developing a cognitive map of the spatial relationships involved.

## cognitive psychology

A branch of psychology that is concerned with the study of internal mental processes such as perception, reasoning, **concept formation**, learning, using language, and making decisions. It is often associated with **information processing** models of cognition. The word *cognition* derives from Latin *cognitus* 'to know, to become acquainted with'.

## cognitive therapy

See **cognitive behaviour modification**

## collective unconscious

A central term in **Jungian** theory: that inherited part of the

**unconscious** which is shared by all members of the human race; also called the **racial unconscious**. It is not related to any personal or individual characteristics, but originates in the evolution of the human brain over centuries. The contents of the collective unconscious are the **archetypes** – universal primordial images that appear in our dreams and in the religious symbols and imagery of differing cultures through the ages.

## combat fatigue

Psychological disturbance caused by the **stress** of being involved in warfare; also called *battle fatigue*. The symptoms are: hypersensitivity to noise and movement, with an exaggerated startle reaction; **anxiety** and irritability; and sleep disturbances, including insomnia and nightmares. The terms date from World War II, but the condition is identical to that known as *shell shock* in World War I, and the symptoms are also similar to those shown by civilians who have been involved in any extremely stressful experience.

See also **gross stress reaction; post-traumatic stress disorder**

## community psychology

A branch of **applied psychology** using theory from **clinical psychology** and **social psychology** to treat problems within a community. This sometimes involves utilizing community resources in order to improve the environment for members of the community who have psychological problems. More often it is aimed at solving problems and improving the quality of life for all members of the community, particularly in areas such as social welfare, education, and relationships between different groups within the community.

## compensation

A term used with slightly different emphasis in differing types of **psychoanalytic** theory, but always with the underlying idea of making up for deficiencies in one area by developing strengths in another. In **Freudian** theory it is presented as a **defence mechanism** which people use to prevent their deficiencies from reaching consciousness. It is also a central idea in the **Adlerian** theory of **personality** to describe the way in which people deal with feelings of inferiority and failure by self-assertion, achievement, and the exercise of power. When the efforts at compensation are more than is required, *overcompensation* takes place, and a person may, for example, become overbearing and aggressive.

See also **inferiority complex**

## complex

As a noun, with the stress on the first syllable, a term in **psychoanalysis**. It refers to a group of repressed and emotionally charged memories and ideas which are in conflict with a person's other ideas and come to exercise a strong influence on the **personality** and behaviour. The word was first used in this way by Jung, but was also used by Freud (eg **castration complex, Oedipus complex**) and Adler (**inferiority complex**).

## compulsion

An irresistible need to engage in behaviour that is often contrary to a person's **conscious** wishes and against that person's interests. The behaviour is usually irrational and often repetitive, and is long-term rather than sudden.

See also **obsession; obsessive-compulsive disorder**

## concept formation

The process by which people come to abstract the essential properties and qualities of the things that they experience and sort them into general rules and classes. Although the term is sometimes used of animals, concept formation is usually thought to be a peculiar function of human **cognitive development** and linked to the use of language. The term generally covers both the acquisition of concepts and the way people learn how to apply them.

## concrete operations

In **Piagetian** theory, the cognitive behaviour and ability characteristic of children between the ages of about 7 to 11. At this stage the child is capable of logical thinking, but only about the concrete physical world; abstract thinking is not yet achievable.

See also **conservation**

## conditioned response

A response which has been learned through a process of **conditioning**. It is properly used only of **classical conditioning**, where the conditioned response is elicited by a previously neutral *conditioned stimulus*. In the classic Pavlovian experiments the conditioned response was the dogs' salivation when they heard the bell that they had come to associate with food. The term is also used sometimes in **operant conditioning**, where it is applied to a response that has been learned through **reinforcement** – for example, turning left in a maze, having learned to do so after having been repeatedly rewarded with food.

## conditioned stimulus

See **classical conditioning**.

## conditioning

In **experimental psychology**, learning in humans or animals which takes place under experimental conditions, and in which the subject learns to respond in a certain way to a stimulus. It is generally divided into **classical conditioning** and **operant conditioning**. In the former, the subject learns to respond to a neutral stimulus that has been associated with another stimulus which would naturally produce this response (the dog salivating when it hears the bell that has previously accompanied food). In the latter, the subject learns to respond in a certain way after its natural response is followed by **reinforcement** (the rat learning to press a bar after being rewarded with food for doing so).

The term can be used in a looser way to describe similar learning that occurs outside the experimental situation. For example, a child who has been given a series of painful injections by a doctor in a white coat might become conditioned to cry at the sight of a woman in a white coat. Parents who praise and reward their toddler for defecating into a potty are hoping to condition the child into eventually using the potty regularly without the reward.

## confusion

A term used by psychologists as in normal English usage, but which in recent years has also come to be used by professionals working with old people as a euphemism for **dementia**. Thus residents in an old people's home or geriatric ward might be described by staff as confused, when they are suffering severe memory loss, are prone to wander off, have personality changes, etc.

## conscious

A term used in the normal sense of being aware of the environment, having sensations and feelings, and reacting to stimuli. In **psychoanalysis**, the conscious is the area of mental activity that one is aware of, as opposed to the **preconscious** and the **unconscious**.

## consensual validation

In **social psychology**, the procedure of assessing the validity of an experience or opinion according to how many other people agree on it. If a lot of people support a particular view, that view becomes more acceptable or valid to others. Likewise if a lot of people claim to have had the same experience or perception, then it is regarded as more likely to be real.

## conservation

The understanding that an object remains the same even when it has undergone some transformation in its appearance. It is important in **Piagetian theory**, as being characteristic of the child at the **concrete operations** stage of mental development. Before this stage children who see a quantity of water being poured from a tall narrow glass to a short wide one will think that there is less water in the short glass, because the surface of the water appears lower down in the glass. At the concrete operations stage, the child has learnt that the quantity of water is constant whatever the shape of the container it is displayed in, that there is still the same amount of cake after it has been cut into slices, and so on.

## convergent thinking

Thinking, particularly associated with problem solving, where the approach is the conventional one of bringing together all the relevant knowledge and information and applying it directly to the problem, on the assumption that there is only one correct answer.
See also **divergent thinking**

## conversion hysteria

In **psychoanalysis**, a disorder in which psychic conflict is converted into physical symptoms, often quite dramatic ones like paralysis; also known as **hysterical conversion, conversion disorder**, or **conversion reaction**. It is characteristic that the patient derives a **secondary gain** from the symptoms, and also that the symptoms correspond to the patient's understanding of his or her physiological make-up, rather than to the actual organic system (eg a paralysis of the foot might correspond to the area covered by a shoe rather than the area that includes the relevant nerve system).

## coping

A term used, particularly in **counselling**, with the normal meaning of dealing with and attempting to overcome problems. Counselling often concentrates on developing or teaching coping techniques or strategies to help the client to deal with problems or anxieties, usually by tackling the source of the problem as opposed to trying to ignore it or using **defence mechanisms**.

## counselling

The process of guiding people, either individually or in groups, to make decisions and solve personal problems by giving advice and information, engaging in therapeutic discussion and activities, administering psychological tests, etc. Counselling services are often specialized: **vocational counselling**, family counselling, etc. There is often a thin dividing line between counselling and **psychotherapy** or various branches of **applied psychology**. However, while **psychotherapists** and **psychologists** are invariably professionals, counsellors in some areas – particularly such as marriage guidance or bereavement counselling – are often volunteers who have completed a training course.
See also **co-counselling**

## counter-phobic character
See **phobic character**

## counter-transference

In **psychoanalysis**, the analyst's **transference** on to the patient, which is thought to be a disturbing element that might distort the course of the analysis. The term is also used more generally to refer to the analyst's feelings and **attitudes** towards the patient, and emotional involvement in the treatment. In this sense, counter-transference does not have the negative effects attributed to the strict interpretation of the term, and is seen as normal and possibly helpful.

### crisis intervention

Short-term **counselling** or **psychotherapy** that is directed towards helping people in an acute situation of psychological stress, such as having attempted or contemplated suicide, having been the victim of rape or domestic violence, or suffering from the effects of drug or alcohol abuse. Crisis intervention is often dealt with by telephone hot-lines or drop-in centres, usually staffed by volunteers.

### critical period

See **sensitive period**

### cryptomnesia

Literally 'hidden memory', from Greek *kryptos* 'secret, hidden' + *mneme* 'memory'. It is applied to a person's thoughts and ideas which appear to be entirely new and creative, but which actually arise from memories of past experience that are not consciously recollected.

### culture-free test

A psychological test, particularly in **educational psychology**, which is designed to be free of all cultural bias, so as to eliminate any advantages or disadvantages derived from belonging to a particular ethnic or socioeconomic group. Such tests (sometimes called *culture-fair tests*) usually minimize language skills and culture-based factual knowledge. It is widely believed that it is impossible to devise a test that is genuinely culture-free.

# D

### dance therapy

The use of dance as an aid to therapy. Folk dancing, disco dancing, or exercises to music are usually used, and self-expression is more relevant than developing artistic skills. It is most often used in the treatment of disturbed children.

### death instinct

In **psychoanalysis**, a **drive** towards destruction and death, evidenced by **aggression**, self-destructive behaviour, and denying oneself pleasure. In **Freudian** theory it is always opposed to the **life instinct**, and is also known as *Thanatos*, pronounced /'θænətɒs/, the name for the Greek god of death. It also holds an important place in **Kleinian** theory, where aggression is regarded as a **projection** of the instinct towards self-destruction.

### death wish

Not really a technical term in psychology, although it is sometimes used to refer to the **death instinct**. It is more often used loosely to suggest an unconscious **motivation** towards death, typically shown by people seeking out dangerous situations and activities.

### defence mechanism

A term first used by Freud, and used by him to describe the unconscious activity of the **ego** in protecting itself from threatening thoughts, memories, or external situations that tend to provoke **anxiety**. The term is also used more generally for any patterns of thought or behaviour that are unconsciously adopted as a defence against anxiety or threats to a person's **self-esteem**. There are many different terms for different types of defence mechanism, including **denial, projection**, and **repression**.

### déjà vu /deɪʒɑ: vu:/ or /vju:/

The common **illusion** that a new experience or scene has been experienced or witnessed before; from French, 'already seen'. Variations of this phenomenon are *déjà pensé* /deɪʒɑ: pãseɪ/ –

'already thought' – and *déjà entendu* /deɪʒɑː ɑ̃tɑ̃ˈduː/ – 'already heard'. The phenomena have been recognized for centuries and there have been many different explanations. In ancient Greek times, it was thought to be evidence of previous incarnations, and this theory has been held by many since, although not by many psychologists. One of the more serious theories is that the illusion is produced by forgotten memories of very similar situations. However, the most commonly held explanation now relates the phenomena to a sort of 'short circuit' in the brain's memory function.

### delusions

In **psychiatry**, false beliefs that are persistently held in the face of evidence and logical argument that contradict them. They are to be distinguished from both **hallucinations** and **illusions**. *Delusions of grandeur* and of *persecution* are often found in **schizophrenic** patients. Some severely depressed patients have *delusions of unworthiness*, often believing that they are guilty of some crime. *Delusions of reference* are delusions where patients pathologically interpret all remarks that they hear as having reference to themselves. Obviously there is a cultural element in diagnosis. Religious beliefs that appear impervious to logical or scientific analysis are not classed as delusions, because they are so widely held.

### dementia

Applied to various disorders that involve a significant impairment of higher mental functions such as memory, reasoning, decision making, and learning. This is usually accompanied by changes in personality and approaches to social interaction. Dementia is often associated with old age (**senile dementia**), but other forms are related to alcohol abuse and multiple concussions (as seen in 'punch-drunk' boxers). All are caused by various forms of cerebral damage or atrophy.
See also **Alzheimer's disease**

### denial

A **defence mechanism** by which the existence of painful or **anxiety**-provoking thoughts, facts, or experiences are simply denied. This does not involve conscious lying or dismissal of painful ideas, but is an **unconscious** operation whereby intolerable thoughts or emotions are disavowed, or an unpleasant experience is not recognized as having taken place.

## dependence

A term used in a variety of different ways. *Drug dependence* has largely replaced *drug addiction* to denote a strong desire or compulsion to continue taking a drug. Drug dependence is usually designated either physiological or psychological. The former, as in dependence on opiates or barbiturates, suggests that the repeated use of a drug has caused physiological alterations and that severe physical symptoms would result if the drug were withdrawn. Psychological dependence is applied to dependence on drugs such as cannabis that do not cause any physical changes.

Dependence is used in **psychiatry** in terms such as *dependent personality disorder* to denote an abnormal reliance on another person or people, to the extent of being unable to make any independent decisions. In **psychoanalysis** it refers to the child's helplessness and dependence on the parent, and to the adult's continued **fixation** on the parents. *Oral dependence* refers to an adult's desire to return to the comfort and security of being suckled. In **social psychology** dependence is an excessive reliance on others to support one's opinions and views of reality.

The word *dependency* is sometimes used instead of dependence in all of the above senses.

## depression

One of the most common psychiatric disorders. The term is used popularly for ordinary 'down' moods, experienced by most people sometimes. It is only used as a diagnostic term in **psychiatry** when the feelings are extreme and long-lasting. The main symptoms are feelings of sadness, despondency, pessimism, inadequacy, and low **self-esteem**, together with a general lethargy and reduction in response and activity. Depression is sometimes, but not always, accompanied by **anxiety**. A clinical division is often made between *reactive* and *endogenous depression*. In the former, the cause of depression is some event in a person's life, such as bereavement, but the depressive reaction is more intense than a normal reaction to a distressing event. The latter term refers to a form of depression with no known apparent precipitating cause.

There is much controversy as to whether depression is caused by inner conflicts and problems or by a biochemical malfunction of the brain. Treatment reflects the controversy, with those who believe that depression has its roots in psychological problems advocating **psychotherapy**, and those who believe it to have physiological causes advocating **drug therapy** or **electroconvulsive therapy**.

## desensitization

A term used similarly to **habituation** to mean any decrease in sensitivity to a stimulus after frequent exposure, more often used for a technique of **behaviour modification**, also called *desensitization procedure* or *systematic desensitization*, which has the aim of reducing **anxiety**, particularly in patients with **phobias**. The technique involves relaxing the patient and then exposing him or her to approximations of the anxiety-producing object, gradually coming nearer and nearer to the actual object, until the patient's anxiety disappears. For example, a patient with a phobia about spiders would be relaxed, perhaps by listening to soothing music in a pleasant environment, and then presented with a picture of a small spider, and encouraged to look at it and eventually touch it. When the patient was able to tolerate this with no anxiety, the therapist would progress to pictures of larger spiders, then models of spiders, then a small live spider, and progressively on until the patient can handle large live spiders without experiencing anxiety.

## developmental psychology

A branch of **psychology** that is concerned with the psychological, physical, cognitive, and social changes that take place throughout a person's life. Whereas once the term covered the entire life-span, it came to be associated solely with development in childhood and adolescence, and to be virtually synonymous with **child psychology**.

## developmental stages

Divisions of the human developmental process which are characterized by certain behaviours, mental abilities, etc. The theories that describe such stages (known as *stage theories*) vary from **Piagetian theory**, which describes the progressive stages of a child's **cognitive development**, to **Freudian** theories of psychosexual development from **oral stage** to **anal stage** to **genital stage**. The German-born psychoanalyst Erik Erikson (1902– ) had a theory of the 'stages of man': eight stages from **basic trust** v **mistrust** in infancy to ego integrity v despair in old age. Other theories concentrate on sensory-motor development and the development of morality.

## differential psychology
See **individual psychology**

## disorganized schizophrenia
See **hebephrenia**

## displacement
A term used in various ways to mean the substitution of one response or piece of behaviour for another. Psychologists studying animal behaviour coined the term *displacement activity* to describe apparently irrelevant behaviour produced by animals in conflict situations, for example, grooming themselves when faced with an aggressive rival. This is sometimes extended to similar behaviour in humans. Displacement also applies to the shifting of emotions from their original object to a more suitable, or less threatening, one. In **psychoanalysis**, the emphasis is on the redirection of feelings from one mental image to another, which is manifested in symbolism in dreams.

## dissociation
In **psychiatry** and **psychotherapy**, the situation in which a set of mental processes, activities, or emotions becomes separated from the rest of a person's personality and functions independently of it. The memory in **amnesia** is dissociated. Extreme forms occur in what are known as *dissociative disorders*, which generally involve a breakdown in the integrity of the personality, and loss of a sense of personal reality.
See also **multiple personality; splitting**

## divergent thinking
Thinking, particularly in connection with problem solving, that is open-ended and flexible in its approach. Ideas diverge, or move off in various directions, in order to encompass all the dimensions of a problem and a wide variety of possible solu-

tions. Divergent thinking is considered to be creative and imaginative, as opposed to the conventional and logical approach of **convergent thinking**.

## Don Juanism
See **satyriasis**

## double-bind

A situation in which someone is faced with conflicting messages from another person in a position of power over him or her, and is unable to find any course of action that will satisfy that person. It is typically used of the relationship between a child and parent, where the parent's emotional demands on the child are incompatible and confusing. The child's overtures of affection may always be repulsed but then whenever the child withdraws its affection, the parent will demand it. Some theorists believe that the stress and confusion caused to a child caught in a double-bind situation may cause **schizophrenia** in later life.

## double blind

A technique in **experimental psychology**. In a double-blind experiment, neither the subject nor the person actually administering the test or procedure knows the relevant facts about the experimental situation. For example, in a double-blind experiment to test the effects of a particular drug on the behaviour of hyperactive children, neither the children nor the experimenter would be told which children have been given the drug and which a placebo. The point of this is to avoid both the **placebo effect** and **experimenter bias**.

## draw-a-person test

A test used with young children, either to test **intelligence** or **personality**. In the *Goodenough Draw-a-Man Test* (sometimes now called *Goodenough Draw-a-Person Test*), children are asked to draw a person as well as they can. The child's intelligence is assessed according to the accuracy and detail of the picture. The *Machover Draw-a-Person Test* is a **projective technique** in which children are asked to draw a person and then tell a story about the person. Children's responses are analysed in order to gain information about their personality, especially their **self-concept**.

### dream analysis

In **psychoanalysis**, the technique whereby the patient's dreams are analysed for their underlying meaning. Typically the patient relates the content of the dream and then uses **free association** in an attempt to interpret the dream. **Freudian** theory holds that dreams are essentially **wish-fulfilment**, but that as wishes and desires are repressed the **unconscious** disguises them by using **symbols, censorship**, and other techniques. The unconscious process whereby the raw material of dreams is transformed into the dream that the patient experiences is known as *dream work*. Dream analysis or *dream interpretation* is the opposite of dream work, as it seeks to reveal the 'real' meaning of the dream.

See also **latent content; manifest content**

### drive

A general term, used for both humans and animals, to mean a strong urge that demands satisfaction. The term *need* is often used more or less synonymously, but some theorists believe that drive is to be distinguished from need in that need does not necessarily imply a **motivation** to satisfy the state of deprivation. Need states are therefore thought to produce drive states.

See also **acquired drive; primary drive**

### drug dependence

See **dependence**

### drug therapy

The use of drugs in treatment. In the treatment of psychiatric disorders the main groups of drugs used are: *sedatives*, usually barbiturates, to reduce insomnia; *tranquillizers*, which reduce **anxiety** and alleviate the symptoms of severe **behaviour disorders**; *anti-depressants*, which alleviate the symptoms of **depression**; *stimulants*, including amphetamines, which are sometimes used to treat obesity, **hyperactivity**, and **narcolepsy**; and *anti-mania drugs*, primarily lithium, used in the treatment of **mania** and **manic depression**.

### dual personality

See **multiple personality**

## dyslexia

An impairment in reading ability, from the Greek prefix *dys-*
'bad, difficult' + *lexis* 'word'. The subject of dyslexia is sur-
rounded by controversy, and educators, psychologists, and
others are by no means agreed as to what constitutes the
condition and how it is to be classified. However, it is generally
thought that dyslexia is a **learning disability** characterized by a
failure to learn to read despite adequate intelligence and
teaching, and where there is no brain damage or other physical, emotional, or cultural factors that might interfere with the
learning process. People with dyslexia find it difficult to see any
order in the written word, and often make reversal errors (eg
reading *b* for *d, god* for *dog*).
See also **reading disability**

## dysphasia

See **aphasia**

# E

### eating disorders

A general term that embraces all serious disorders marked by a
disturbance in eating habits and appetites. The most common
such disorders are **anorexia nervosa** and **bulimia**. *Pica* /'paɪkə/
(the word is Latin for 'magpie') is an eating disorder characterized by a craving for unusual and unnatural foods – anything
from earth to coal to soap. It is sometimes found temporarily in
pregnancy and in young children, but is more often a symptom
of psychological disturbance.

### echolalia /ɛkəˈleɪlɪə/

The involuntary and senseless repetition of words or phrases
that someone else has just said; derived from *echo* + Greek *lalia*
'talk'; also sometimes called **echophrasia**. It is often the result of
brain damage, but is also found in **autism** and various severe
psychological disorders.

### ECT

See **electroconvulsive therapy**.

### educational psychology

The branch of **psychology** that is concerned with theories and
problems of teaching and study. It covers such topics as learning
theories, the assessment of **ability** and **aptitude**, principles of
teacher training, and all aspects of psychology concerned with
learning and with children and their social and **cognitive
development**, as applied in an educational environment.

### ego

A term used in its most general sense to indicate what people
mean by 'I', the self, the part of human personality that one is
consciously aware of; from Latin, 'I'. This is extended by some
to mean all the psychological processes of thought and emotion
and interaction with the world that are concerned with the self,
and there is often a suggestion of an excessive concern with self,
as in **egocentrism** and egotism. However, the term is most

significant as an essential part of **Freudian** theory. According to this theory, the ego is one of the three components of a person's psychic apparatus, the others being the **id** and the **superego**. The ego represents the **conscious** processes of thought, memory, and perception that are most in touch with reality. Its function is to act as a sort of executive or mediator, maintaining a balance between the id's demands and desires and the superego's restrictions and prohibitions. It does this by operating **defence mechanisms**.

### egocentrism

Literally, being centred around the 'I', or self. When used of adults it is meant in the ordinary sense of preoccupation with the self, being self-absorbed and uninterested in the interests and concerns of others. When used of children, the term usually refers to the **Piagetian theory** of child development, in which egocentrism is a natural stage, lasting until a child is 7 or 8. At this stage, a child sees everything from its own point of view and is unable to conceive how things appear to others, or how other people might be affected by events or situations in a different way from itself. The child's speech and thought reflect this limited conceptual world that revolves around the self.

### ego ideal

A term used in **Freudian** theory to mean the **ego**'s ideal or model, to which it would wish to conform. Simply, it can be seen as the positive standards and ambitions that represent what a person would like to be. The ego ideal is formed through **identification** with the parents or parent figures or substitutes who are admired. It differs from the **superego** in that it is positive rather than negative: it prescribes good thoughts and behaviour rather than banning bad thoughts and behaviour. Failure to conform to the ego ideal produces shame and a sense of inferiority rather than guilt.

### ego psychology

(1) The psychology of the **ego** and its specific functions, as outlined by Freud. (2) A school of post-Freudian psychoanalytic theory, in which greater emphasis is put on the ego and its functions in connection with personality development and external reality.

## Electra complex

A **Jungian** term for the female equivalent of the **Oedipus complex**. Jung coined the term from the Greek story of Electra who avenged her father's death by helping her brother to murder her mother. Freud rejected the term, as he did not believe that the girl's attachment to her father and rivalry with her mother was actually analogous to the boy's Oedipus complex. It is now rarely used; the complex in females is included in the term *Oedipus complex*.

## electric shock therapy

See **electroconvulsive therapy**

## electroconvulsive therapy (ECT)

Treatment for severe **depression** involving the use of electric current to induce shock; often called **electric shock therapy**. The patient is sedated and given a muscle relaxant to prevent physical injury, then electrodes are placed at the temples, a weak electric current is passed through the brain, and a convulsive seizure takes place. The treatment is usually given two or three times a week for anything from two to six weeks. The therapy was originally based on the theory (since disproved) that epileptics never suffer from depression, so experiencing fits might cure depression. At one time the therapy was very widely used and often abused, in that patients were given too many sessions; in some mental institutions, its use was often punitive.

Insofar as the treatment works, it is still not known why it does; there are often side-effects of memory loss and confusion; and there has been a backlash against former abuse of the therapy. However, electroconvulsive therapy is still quite widely used, although much more cautiously than in the past, and is normally reserved for severely depressed patients who have failed to respond to anti-depressive drugs.

## emotion

A word used in so many ways in psychology that it defies clear definition; from Latin *exmovere* 'to disturb, stir up'. It is generally used to speak of subjectively experienced states of strong feeling which are either pleasant or unpleasant – eg love, tenderness, hatred, envy, anger, fear – and which are usually accompanied by physiological changes. They are thought of as intense, acute, and relatively short-lived states of arousal which motivate people to action. There are any number of psychological theories connected with emotion, and the experiencing of inappropriate emotion or emotional reaction is a feature of many forms of psychiatric disorder.

## empathy

The ability to understand and be sensitive to the feelings, ideas, and actions of another person, although not actually experiencing the same feelings. It can be looked at as putting oneself into another's shoes, while wholly retaining one's own identity. Empathy is considered to be an essential quality for those practising **counselling** and **psychotherapy**. The term, modelled on the word **sympathy**, was coined in the early 1900s as an equivalent of the German *Einfühlung*, which previously had no exact English translation.

## encounter group

See **sensitivity training**

## endogenous depression

See **depression**

## engulfment

In **Laingian** psychology, **anxiety** experienced by those who are lacking in a firm sense of their own autonomous identity, and for whom all relationships with others are threats to the identity. Such people see love and affection from others as more disturbing than hatred, for they fear being engulfed or swallowed up by the other person's love, and somehow being absorbed into the person and losing their own identity.

## envy

A term used with its standard meaning, but also with specialized meaning for some theorists. The British-born psychologist William McDougall (1871–1938) defined envy as 'a grudging contemplation of more fortunate people' and 'a binary compound of negative self-feeling and of anger'. Envy is an important concept in **Kleinian** theory, in which the infant's ambivalent feelings towards the mother's breast are thought to be central to its psychic development. The child is said to have an innate envy of the mother's breast and its creativity. Envy is to be distinguished from **jealousy**, in which a third party is involved.

See also **penis envy**

## Eros

The Greek god of love. In **Freudian** theory, Eros is used to symbolize the **life instinct**, in the same way that the god of death, Thanatos, symbolizes the **death instinct**. Eros is used variously in Freud's writings as a symbol of sexual or erotic love, to refer to all the life-preserving instincts, and as a synonym for **libido**.

## ESP

See **extrasensory perception**

## EST

(1) /i: ɛs ti:/ An abbreviation of **electric shock therapy**. (2) /ɛst/ An acronym for **Erhard Seminar Training**. EST is a form of **group therapy** based on the theories of the American Werner Erhard (1935– ), who was influenced by various sources, mainly related to the **human potential movement**, including Zen Buddhism, Scientology, and positive thinking philosophies. It involves very large group sessions of long duration, where people are subjected to physical discomfort, meditation, and very intense therapy aimed at individual fulfilment and getting **in touch** with their sense of personal responsibility. Erhard's background was in selling, and his system is criticized by many who see it as a heavily marketed mass religion rather than a therapeutic process, and one that could be dangerous for those with genuine psychological disturbances.

## ethnocentrism

The disposition to regard all other races, cultures, and ethnic groups from the standpoint of one's own culture; from Greek *ethnos* 'race, people' + *centre*. It resembles **egocentrism** in that it involves a failure to identify with the viewpoint or interests of any other group than one's own, and almost always carries the implication that one's own race or cultural group is superior to all others.

## exceptional children

In **educational psychology** and **child psychology**, children who are atypical because of giftedness, physical or mental handicap, emotional or learning difficulties, etc. The term originates in the USA, where it was thought that a category that included those who needed special education because of giftedness or high intelligence would help to remove the stigma from those who needed it because of handicap or low intelligence. In the UK, the term *children with special needs* is more often used.

## exchange theory

A theory of **social psychology** that conceptualizes relationships between people in terms of economic transactions; also known as *social exchange theory*. It is based on the principle that people balance the cost of their social interactions against their expectations of gain or return from them. As applied to friendship and close relationships, the theory is that people make an estimation of their own personal worth or value and seek friendship with those whom they estimate as having a similar value.

## existential psychology

Any psychological theory that has its roots in existentialist philosophy, a movement that emphasizes the individual's free will and responsibility for choices in a world that is essentially unfathomable. Existential psychology rejects theories of **unconscious** causation for human behaviour, and prefers to study the **conscious** mind and its experiences.

## existential therapy

**Psychotherapy** based on **existential psychology**. It rejects the belief that the client in therapy is a sick person and that the therapist's task is to effect a cure, but works on the principle that the therapist should help the client to analyse his or her **conscious** self and immediate reality, and reach a position of self-awareness.

## experimental neurosis

In **experimental psychology**, the 'neurotic' behaviour shown by animals in certain experimental situations. It was coined by Pavlov, who conditioned dogs to salivate when they saw a circle but not an ellipse. Gradually he changed the shape of the ellipse

so that it became increasingly circular, and it became impossible for the dogs to discriminate between circle and ellipse. They then showed signs of disturbed behaviour, barking wildly, biting the equipment, etc. Rats who were given electric shocks whenever they attempted to eat or drink also showed signs of extreme disturbance. There is much controversy as to whether it is appropriate to speak of **neurosis** in animals, and whether the behaviour of animals in these experimental situations can be applied in any way to humans.
See also **classical conditioning**

## experimental psychology
A general term for all approaches to psychological issues that use experimental methods. It was previously applied only to psychological research that actually took place in laboratories and frequently involved animals, but is now used much more widely for all psychological research that involves the experimental method of manipulating variables. Areas where experimental methods are particularly appropriate are those connected with learning, memory, perception, and **motivation**, but most branches of psychology include experimental aspects.

## experimenter bias
The effect that the beliefs and expectations of the experimenter can have on the results of the experiment. It is thought that most experimenters make predictions about the outcome of an experiment, and either consciously or unconsciously seek to influence the proceedings so that the outcome will conform to their expectations. This can often introduce a bias into the experiment.
See also **double-blind; Rosenthal effect; self-fulfilling prophecy**

## externalization
A term with diverse meanings, but all conveying the idea of something that is internal becoming external. In **developmental psychology** it refers to the child's gradual awareness of itself as opposed to the external world, and its separation of its sense of self from things external to self. In **social psychology** and some theories of **personality**, externalization refers to attributing the causes of one's thoughts and behaviour to some outside

agency. In **psychoanalysis** it is often used synonymously with **projection**.

## extinction

A term connected with **conditioning** and referring to the weakening of a **conditioned response**. In **classical conditioning** this happens when the conditioned stimulus is constantly presented with no unconditioned stimulus present (eg the bell is rung but no food accompanies it). In **operant conditioning**, extinction occurs when **reinforcement** constantly fails to accompany the conditioned response (eg the rat presses the lever but no food appears).

## extrasensory perception (ESP)

Perception that takes place without the use of the known sensory processes. It includes such abilities as thought transference, clairvoyance, and **telepathy**, but the genuine existence of these phenomena is a matter of controversy among psychologists.
See also **parapsychology**

## extravert

A term in wide general use, but actually part of the **Jungian** theory of **personality**; literally, a person who is turned outside of him/herself, from Latin *extra* 'outside' + *vertere* 'to turn'. The spelling *extrovert*, formed on the analogy of *introvert*, is also acceptable. According to Jung's theory of personality types, the extravert is characterized by being outgoing, responsive to others, gregarious, and impulsive, interested in the events and experiences of the outside world rather than in his or her own mental state. The extravert is sociable and confident in unfamiliar company and surroundings. However, the extreme extravert can be overdependent on group acceptance and can be aggressive when encountering opposition. Jung's idea of a polar distinction between extraversion and introversion has been largely discredited, as psychologists have realized that most people come somewhere in between these extremes or have elements of both extraversion and introversion, displayed at different times.
See also **introvert**

# F

## face-to-face group

In **social psychology**, a small group of people gathered for discussion or other purposes, and seated in close enough physical proximity for each member of the group to be able to interact with every other member. The optimum number for such a group is probably five or six, and the maximum eight.

## facilitation

Literally, 'making easier'. The term is used in a variety of ways in psychology. Its most technical use is in relation to the transmission of nerve impulses, where facilitation involves lowering the threshold for conduction along a neural pathway. *Reproductive facilitation* refers to the facilitation of learning, by interposing some quite unrelated activity between the learning and the time the material is to be recalled or reproduced. In **experimental psychology** facilitation refers to the strengthening of a response by repeated stimulation.

However, the word is now most frequently used in a non-technical sense in **psychotherapy**, and particularly in **counselling**. In this area facilitation is often thought to be the therapist's principal task: enabling clients to become aware of the nature of their problems and the choices before them, and helping them to make their own decisions about what choices and changes to make in their lives. Therapists and counsellors who have this non-directive approach (see **client-centred therapy; non-directive counselling**) often refer to themselves as *facilitators*, both in relation to individual and group therapy or counselling. This terminology has made its way into small-group work of all kinds, not necessarily therapeutic, where it has become fashionable for group leaders to be known as facilitators.

See also **social facilitation**

## family therapy

**Psychotherapy** which involves treating the entire family rather than an individual member. Family therapy sometimes differs in emphasis from family **counselling**, in which it is usually assumed that the whole family is involved in a particular problem and needs to sort it out together with a counsellor's help. In family therapy there is usually one family member who presents with the problem, but the therapist believes that the whole family should be regarded as the object of therapy. Some therapists think that the illness of the individual member is caused by disturbed relationships within the family; others actually consider the individual's illness as a symptom of the **neurosis** of the whole family.

## fantasy

The process of creating images and events in the imagination, usually related to one's **wish-fulfilment**. Fantasies are usually produced spontaneously, and indulging in fantasy is regarded as normal and even psychologically healthy. It is only a problem when fantasy becomes more important than real life to a person, or when it is related to **delusions** or drug abuse. In **psychoanalysis**, fantasy occurs either in **conscious** daydreams or **unconscious** imaginings which are revealed in **dream analysis**. There is some controversy over the spelling of the term. The English word derives from *fancy*, and because it has acquired connotations of whimsy and fancifulness, some psychoanalytic writers prefer the spelling *phantasy*, which relates to the German *Phantasie* 'imagination', and therefore seems more appropriate. The spelling *phantasy* is most common with British writers, but *fantasy* is more often used in the USA.

## father figure

Someone who takes the place of a father and fulfils the psychological functions of a father for an individual. Usually in a position of authority, he becomes the male figure that the individual identifies with, looks to for approval, and conceptualizes in his or her internal image of a father. The term is sometimes applied to a stepfather, foster father, or other person who has actually taken over a father's role, but some use the term *father surrogate* for such a person. More typically a father figure is someone who has assumed this role in the eyes of the individual concerned, but who may not even be aware that he is regarded in this way.

## fear

An **emotion** evoked by present or anticipated danger, and characterized by physiological changes, a subjective experience of unpleasantness and agitation, and the desire to flee, attack, or hide. Psychologists differentiate fear from **anxiety**, which is more general and undifferentiated, and **phobia**, which is essentially irrational.

## fear of failure/success

*Fear of failure* means literally what it says: a condition peculiar to people who feel under pressure to succeed, particularly associated with a high **need for achievement**. *Fear of success* refers to the need to refrain from accomplishing goals and achieving maximum success, because of expectations of negative consequences. The term was coined by the American psychologist Matina Horner (1939– ), who believed that this fear was peculiar to women, who are socialized into believing that success is inappropriate to their sex. It is now accepted that men also suffer from fear of success, and that the phenomenon may be closely linked to its supposed opposite – fear of failure – as success increases challenges and the likelihood of failure.

## fetish

Generally, an object of exaggerated reverence or devotion. It originates in anthropology, where it is used for a totem or object believed to possess magical powers, and derives from Portuguese *feitiço* 'artificial, false'. In **psychiatry** the main use of the term is to describe an inanimate object or part of the body, not in itself erotic, that has become the focus of sexual excitement. *Fetishism* is the condition where a person's sexual arousal is dependent on a fetish. The most common fetishes are items of clothing such as shoes or underwear, or parts of the body such as feet or long hair, and a person with such a fetish is labelled accordingly (eg a *foot fetishist*).

## fixation

A term used in various ways in psychology to describe the process by which something becomes fixed and inflexible. However, the principal meaning is within **psychoanalysis**, where it refers to a persistent attachment to an object or person that is appropriate to an earlier stage of an individual's development. In **Freudian** terms this often relates to the psychosexual **developmental stages,** and a person may be said to be fixated at the **oral stage** or **anal stage**. The fixation is often upon a parent (*mother fixation, father fixation*). Fixated adults are thought to be immature and neurotic in that they retain a childish ambivalence towards the object of fixation which colours all their future relationships and prevents them from developing mature **attitudes** towards others.

## flight into health

The phenomenon whereby a patient, faced with the prospect of **psychotherapy,** suddenly appears to recover completely. It is assumed to be a **defence mechanism** designed to avoid the often painful self-examination that is central to many forms of psychotherapy.

## flight into illness

The development of symptoms as a means of escaping or avoiding conflict. It was originally a **Freudian** term, and referred specifically to patients in analysis developing new neurotic symptoms as a **defence mechanism** to avoid examining the central conflicts in their lives. The idea has been extended to illness in general, and is used to describe the way people in situations of conflict develop illnesses as an escape. See also **primary gain; secondary gain**

## flooding

See **implosion therapy**

## focal therapy

A restricted form of **psychotherapy**. Instead of dealing with the whole of the patient's life, relationships, and problems, only the specific problem that the person is most concerned with is used as the focus of the therapy. Focal therapy is usually fairly short-term, restricted to a limited number of weekly sessions.

## folie à deux /fɒli æ dɜː/

French, 'madness of two'. It is descriptive of the phenomenon where two people in a close and long-term relationship, often husband and wife or siblings, come to share the same **delusions,** often of a **paranoid** nature.

## formal operations

The mental processes characteristic of the final stage in Piaget's theory of cognitive **developmental stages**. At this stage, beginning at around 12 or 13, children become capable of thought that is not tied to concrete facts and objects. They are able to handle abstract ideas, reason logically, and formulate and test hypotheses.

See also **Piagetian theory**

## free association

A technique in **psychoanalysis** in which patients are encouraged to express freely all the thoughts and images that come into their minds, with no constraints or reservation, no intellectual control or concentration, and no guidance from the therapist. Eventually this will reveal clues to the patient's **unconscious** conflicts. The term is also used for a form of psychological test where subjects have to report the first thought that comes into their head when presented with a stimulus, usually a word or phrase (see **word association test**).

## free-floating anxiety

A vague state of **anxiety** that is not attached to any particular object or event and has no apparent cause. In **psychoanalysis** it is assumed that the anxiety did have a specific source, but has become detached from the original precipitating circumstances and generalized.

## Freudian

Relating to the theories of the Austrian founder of **psychoanalysis**, Sigmund Freud (1856–1939). Freud's work has been enormously influential, not just in the development of psychoanalysis but in the history of 20th-c ideas, and although much of his theory has been modified or challenged by his successors, it remains the basis of much therapeutic practice and terminology. Freud's most important ideas are in the areas of the significance of the **unconscious, dream analysis**, the psychosexual **developmental stages**, the aspects of human **personality**, and the theory that mental disturbance is rooted in early experience and that the analytic therapeutic process can effect explanation, interpretation, and eventually change. The term *classical theory* is sometimes used as a synonym for Freudian theory.

## Freudian slip

A popular term for what in **Freudian** theory is called *parapraxis*, literally 'faulty action'. It refers to small mistakes of speech or behaviour in areas where a person would not normally make errors and which are due to the intrusion of repressed **unconscious** wishes or conflicts. Although parapraxis includes minor accidents and lapses of memory, the classic manifestations of the Freudian slip are slips of the tongue or pen. For example, someone might say, 'My father's deep in death' instead of 'deep in debt', revealing repressed hostility to their father. Freudian slips are quite a common phenomenon in 'normal' people with no particular mental disorders or problems.

## fugue /fjuːg/

A disturbed state in which a person performs actions apparently consciously, but has no recollection of them afterwards; from Latin, 'flight'. It is used particularly for cases of prolonged **amnesia** where people suddenly leave home and start a new life and a new identity with no memories of their previous life. After they have recovered, they will typically recall their past life and identity but have no memory of what happened during the fugue period.

## functional

A term used in various ways in psychology, with meanings somehow related to function or purpose. In the terms *functional disorder* and *functional psychosis* it means that the disorder is psychological in origin and has no known physical cause. *Functional analysis* is a term used to describe the **Skinnerian** form of **behaviourism**, where behaviour is analysed without any examination of its structure or underlying **motivation**. The term *functional autonomy* is associated with the theory of the American psychologist Gordon Allport (1897–1967), which suggests that behaviour that was originally designed to achieve some goal can lose its dependence on the original motivation and become valuable in itself.

## functionalism

An approach to psychology that concentrates on examining the function and utility of the mind rather than its contents; also known as **functional psychology**. It is thought of as being in opposition to the introspective approach of **structuralism**.

# G

### gender-identity disorder

Failure to identify with the sex to which one is assumed to belong. *Gender identity* means experiencing oneself as being either male or female. In the disorder, there is usually a feeling of inappropriateness and discomfort with one's body and the gender-role expectations of society. In childhood this manifests itself by an overwhelming preference for the clothing, toys, and activities associated with the other sex. It should be emphasized that this preference is extreme and compulsive, and not just the disregard for conformity with gender stereotypes exhibited by many children. In adults it is typically manifested in **transsexualism** and **transvestism**.

### genital character

In **psychoanalysis**, the characteristics of mature psychosexual development, where loving sexual relationships with the opposite sex can be formed. In **Freudian** theory it is assumed that the genital character has successfully worked through and synthesized all the previous psychosexual stages.

### genital stage

A term used in two ways in **psychoanalytic** theory. It is sometimes used of the stage at around 4 or 5 when a child becomes interested in its sexual organs and the differences between the sexes, and forms an attachment to the parent of the opposite sex. This is sometimes regarded as part of the **phallic stage**, and sometimes also called the *Oedipal stage*. More often the term is used of a later stage of psychosexual development, after the **latency period**, when adolescents start to show an interest in the opposite sex, and eventually to form sexual relationships with them.

### Gestalt psychology /gəˈʃtælt/

A German word which defies exact English translation, but means something like 'form' or 'configuration', with the suggestion of a unified whole whose nature is more than the summation of its parts. The basis of Gestalt psychology is that psychological phenomena cannot be understood through the analysis of their composite parts, but must be regarded as a whole. The Gestalt school of psychology began as a reaction to **structuralism**. It has been influential in various areas of psychology, particularly in the field of perception, where it has been recognized that incomplete figures are seen as complete, and that random spots of light are organized into patterns by the viewer, who perceives their underlying unity. Gestalt psychology was also important in the theory of **insight learning**, and in the development of holistic theories of **social psychology** and **personality**.

## Gestalt therapy

A form of **psychotherapy** loosely based on **Gestalt psychology** theories. The approach is holistic and focuses on the totality of an individual's experience and functioning. The aim, both in individual and **group therapy**, is to raise levels of self-awareness and self-acceptance.

## glossolalia

Speaking in tongues; from Greek *glósso* 'tongue' + *lalia* 'talk'. It refers to the utterance of what sounds like a foreign language but is not recognizable as any known language and appears to have no formal linguistic content. This phenomenon is described several times in the New Testament (eg Acts 2.1–4, 19.6; 1 Corinthians 14.1–13). The textbook description of glossolalia often refers to 'religious ecstasy', but speaking in tongues is a normal and accepted aspect of worship in many Christian churches. However, outside of the context of religious worship, it can be a symptom of severe psychological disturbance.

## gross stress reaction

A general term for the sort of reaction, usually of **anxiety**, sleeplessness, etc, that is brought about by experiencing an extremely stressful situation. It includes such disorders as **combat fatigue** and **post-traumatic stress disorder**, but does not apply to the ordinary stress reactions to situations experienced by most people in everyday life.

## group dynamics

In **social psychology**, the interaction of people in groups, and the study of this interaction. It applies mainly to small groups, either arbitrary groupings of people who work or study together or people who have formed into a group for some social, political, therapeutic, or other purpose. The emphasis is on how groups form, the power structures within groups, how leaders emerge, the role that each individual plays in the group, how decisions are made, and how the group relates to other groups.

## group therapy

Any kind of **psychotherapy** conducted with a group rather than with individuals. The principle common to most group therapy is that people can help each other by engaging in group interaction and sharing their experiences, under the guidance of the therapist or group facilitator. Techniques vary greatly, from the sort of mutual self-help and morale raising of an Alcoholics Anonymous or similar group, to the techniques of *group analysis*, where the interactions between members of a small group are interpreted according to **psychoanalytic** theory.

See also **assertiveness training; EST** (2); **family therapy**

## guiding fiction

An **Adlerian** term, referring to the constant internal ideas and principles which form an **unconscious** background to the way people direct and evaluate their experiences and behaviour throughout their lives. The guiding fiction is consistent with reality to a greater or a lesser extent according to the mental health of the individual.

## guilt

A subjective emotional state of being aware of having violated the moral norms or standards of one's family, or religious or social group. Guilt involves regret and not simply fear of punishment, and the offence can be real or imaginary. In **psychoanalysis** the emphasis is on guilt as the result of conflict between the **superego** and a person's sexual and aggressive desires.

See also **survivor guilt**

# H

## habituation

In **experimental psychology**, the waning of a response to a stimulus as a result of its increased familiarity in repeated presentations. This occurs in ordinary life, as well as in the experimental situation. For example, people become habituated to the noise of trains if they live near a railway. The term is also used in relation to drug use to describe psychological **dependence** on a drug.

## hallucination

The apparent perception of an object that is not actually present, or the experience of sensory perceptions with no external cause. Hallucinations are usually thought of as related to 'seeing things' or 'hearing things' (*visual* and *auditory hallucinations*) but any of the senses can be involved (*olfactory, tactile, gustatory hallucinations*). They are generally regarded as a symptom of **psychosis**, except in cases where the hallucination occurs when a person is in the **hypnagogic state** or not properly awake, is in the throes of an ecstatic religious experience, or has been taking hallucinogenic drugs such as LSD or mescaline.

## halo effect

A term in **social psychology**, used particularly in relation to tests where people are asked to rate the **personality** of others. It refers to the tendency to generalize from observing one particular positive or likable trait in someone to evaluating his or her overall personality favourably, or to attribute all kinds of admirable qualities and beliefs to people because we happen to like them. The same term is applied to negative as well as positive instances, ie where someone is considered altogether unlikable because of one unpleasant trait.

## Hawthorne effect

In **social psychology**, the phenomenon of performance or productivity being stimulated merely because people are having attention paid to them and being subjected to experimental innovations; named after the Hawthorne works of the Western Electric Company, where an experimental study was conducted in 1927. The women workers were subjected to a series of changes in their working conditions (hours, rest times, lighting, system of payment, degree of consultation, etc) in order to establish which factors increased their productivity. In fact, whatever changes were introduced, even ones expected to have a negative effect, the women's productivity and output increased. It was concluded that it was the fact of having people appearing concerned about them, and the novelty of the changes, rather than the actual changes in conditions themselves, which caused the increased productivity.

**hebephrenia** /hi:bɪˈfri:nɪə/
One of the most common forms of **schizophrenia**; also known as **hebephrenic schizophrenia** and **disorganized schizophrenia**; from Greek *hebe* 'youth' + *phrenia* 'disorder of the mind'. The 'youth' element does not refer to the age of onset but to the childish behaviour that is characteristic of this disorder. The main symptoms are shallow emotions demonstrated in shows of **inappropriate affect**, erratic speech, silly or bizarre behaviour, withdrawal from reality, **delusions**, and **hallucinations**.

**hedonism** /ˈhɛdənɪzm/ *or* /ˈhi:dənɪzm/
In psychology, the theory that the **motivation** for all behaviour is the pursuit of pleasure and the avoidance of pain; from Greek *hedone* 'pleasure'. This does not carry the implication of the philosophical theory of hedonism, which actually suggests that people *ought* to pursue pleasure and avoid pain.

**heredity-environment controversy**
See **nature-nurture controversy**

**holding**
A non-technical term used a great deal in **psychotherapy** and **counselling**. Therapists talk of being 'held' or feeling 'held' to convey the sense of warmth, security, and acceptance experienced in a close relationship, and reminiscent of the absolute security known by an infant held in its mother's arms.

## holism

The theory that living things cannot be understood through an analysis of their composite parts, but only as a whole. Any form of psychological theory or therapeutic method which proceeds on this basis is described as *holistic*.

## homophobia

An extreme dislike of **homosexuality** and homosexual people. Homophobia is hardly ever a true **phobia**, involving irrational fear, panic symptoms, etc, although its basis usually is irrational. It is more often found in men than in women, and is sometimes related to fear that they might themselves have homosexual tendencies.

## homosexuality

Sexually attraction towards people of the same gender as oneself, from Greek *homos* 'same'. The term is also used to mean sexual activity between people of the same gender. For many years homosexuality was regarded as a **mental illness** or a sexual **perversion**, and there have been various theories as to its causes and possible forms of treatment. It is now fairly generally accepted by professionals in psychology and psychiatry that the majority of homosexuals appear to be born with a predisposition towards homosexuality; that homosexuals are as likely to be as well-balanced as anyone else; and that the only difference between homosexuals and heterosexuals is their sexual orientation, and the culture and lifestyle that tends to accompany it. Female homosexuals are usually known as *lesbians*, from the Greek island of Lesbos, home of the 7th-c BC poet Sappho, whose love poetry was thought to be homosexual.

## hostage transference

See **Stockholm syndrome**

## humanistic psychology

A school of psychology opposed to the theories of both **psychoanalysis** and **behaviourism**. It concentrates on 'normal' rather than 'neurotic' behaviour, and on the qualities that make human beings unique among living things: the capacity for creativity, self-knowledge, humour, aesthetic appreciation, altruism, and psychological growth. Humanistic psychology is

largely associated with the work of the American psychologists
Abraham Maslow (1908–70) and Carl Rogers (1902–87).

## human potential movement

A general term covering various therapeutic methods that are
somehow aimed at improving the individual's self-awareness
and interactions with others. It includes such techniques as
**assertiveness training** and **sensitivity training**, and **EST**.
Many of the methods involved have been adopted for training
personnel in business, public administration, and the armed
forces. However, some people have reservations about the
movement, partly because it usually involves private enterprise
rather than public health services, and partly because of its
tendency to include aspects of unsystematic, mystical, or 'New
Age' approaches such as meditation, yoga, astrology, and Zen
Buddhism.

## hyperactivity

Abnormal or excessive activity, characterized by restlessness,
impulsiveness, and inability to concentrate for any length of
time. It is found in cases of **mania** or in the manic phase of
**manic depression**. However, it is most often used to refer to a
disorder in children, where it is more or less synonymous with
**attention-deficit disorder**, although that term is more common in the USA than in Britain. It affects about one in 200
children, mainly boys.

There have been various theories as to the cause of hyperactivity, varying from emotional disturbance to brain dysfunction to
the recent theory that additives and other elements in food can
have a contributory effect. This last theory is still very contro-
versial, but dramatic results have been achieved by putting
hyperactive children on drastically reformed diets. Danish
researchers have recently found an impairment in the blood
flow to the *corpus striatum* region in the brains of hyperactive
children. This might explain the success of the drug *Ritalin* in
treating hyperactivity, although it is not a tranquillizer but an
amphetamine-based stimulant; it is possible that it stimulates
the flow of blood to the striatum. However, most treatment is
still based on **psychotherapy**, using **behaviour modification**
techniques, and often includes training parents in how best to
cope with their hyperactive children.

## hypermnesia

Literally 'excessive memory'; applied both to memory that is abnormally clear and to the ability to recall an unusual amount of information. An unusual ability to remember facts and figures is sometimes found in people who are not abnormal in any other way, but also occasionally in **idiot savants**. The abnormally clear recall of past experiences and emotions sometimes occurs under **hypnosis**, in the manic phase of **manic depression**, and to the patient in **psychoanalysis**.

## hypnagogic state /hɪpnə'gɒdʒɪk/

The drowsy state experienced just as one is about to fall asleep; from Greek *hypnos* 'sleep' + *agogos* 'leading'. It is not abnormal for people to experience **hallucinations** when in this state.

## hypnosis

A word deriving from *Hypnos*, the Greek god of sleep; but though hypnosis is often defined as 'artificially induced sleep', the hypnotic state is different from sleep in many ways. Hypnosis brings about a state superficially resembling sleep, but without the same physiological characteristics. Hypnotized subjects are extremely suggestible to the hypnotist, they are almost completely passive, and their critical and decision-making faculties are greatly reduced. Their awareness of the environment is limited to what the hypnotist suggests and can be much distorted. Orders given by the hypnotist are obeyed, either during the hypnotic state or after the subject has emerged from it. A *post-hypnotic suggestion* may be acted upon immediately a subject comes out of the trance or a good deal later, and subjects apparently have no recollection that the motivation for their actions originated from the hypnotist. Although there was intense interest in the phenomenon and its therapeutic possibilities among 19th-c and early 20th-c psychologists, it is still not wholly understood, and not widely used by professional psychologists or psychiatrists.
See also **hypnotherapy**

## hypnotherapy

Any form of **psychotherapy** that uses **hypnosis**. Although Freud abandoned the use of hypnotism at an early stage, and went on to develop the classical theories and practices of

**psychoanalysis**, hypnosis is still occasionally used by some psychoanalysts in order to reduce a patient's **resistance** to the analyst's interpretations, or to assist **abreaction**. Otherwise, hypnotherapy focuses on the power of hypnotism to render a person passive and open to suggestions that might change **attitudes** and behaviour. It is more likely to be of help to people with one relatively minor problem, such as the need to give up smoking, than for those with serious psychiatric problems.

## hypochondria

An excessive preoccupation with one's health, and a tendency to interpret very minor symptoms of ill-health as being signs of major diseases; also known as **hypochondriasis**. The term comes from a Greek word referring to the regions on either side of the upper abdomen, under the ribs, which was supposed to be the source of hypochondria. Many people suffer mildly from hypochondria, but it is regarded as a symptom of psychiatric disorder only when the preoccupation with health is extreme and overwhelming, or when the patient's belief that he or she is suffering from an incurable disease amounts to a **delusion**.

## hysteria

A severe psychiatric disorder with a variety of symptoms; from Greek *hystera* 'womb', as it was originally thought that only women suffered from it. The main symptoms are **dissociation, hallucinations**, the presence of physical symptoms with no physiological cause, and various other manifestations including **amnesia**, somnambulism, and facial tics. Hysteria is no longer regarded as a single disorder, and is not used as a diagnostic term. Those with the classic symptoms of what used to be called hysteria might be diagnosed as suffering from a *dissociative disorder* or from a **conversion hysteria**.
See also **dissociation; mass hysteria**

## hysterical contagion
See **mass hysteria**

## hysterical conversion
See **conversion hysteria**

# I

## id

In **Freudian** theory, one of the three agencies of human personality, the others being the **ego** and the **superego**. The id (Latin 'it') is the instinctual and primitive part of the psychic apparatus, containing deep **unconscious** drives related to sex and **aggression**. It is disorganized, isolated from the environment, and dominated by the **pleasure principle**. It is the task of the **ego** to restrain the single-minded desire of the id to fulfil its needs.

## idealization

A term used in two ways in **psychoanalytic** theory. It can mean the elevation of a person or people to an ideal of perfection, refusing to acknowledge any of their negative characteristics. The idealized objects may well be the parents, and there is often **identification** with the exalted image of their perfection. Idealization is partly a refusal to recognize **ambivalence**, and this idea is taken up in the other use of the term. For some theorists, particularly **Kleinian** ones, idealization is a **defence mechanism** involving the **splitting** of an object of ambivalence into two aspects, an ideally good one and an altogether bad one.

## idée fixe /ideɪ fiːks/

French, 'fixed idea'. A persistent irrational idea that is held obsessively, dominates the mind for a long period of time, and is impervious to any logical argument or evidence that proves its indefensibility.

## identification

A term used generally in psychology to refer to the mental act of establishing a close link between oneself and a person, people, or group with which one feels a close emotional bond. In **psychoanalysis** it means the process of assimilating attributes of another person, and taking that person as a pattern. The term *identification with the aggressor* was coined by Anna Freud (Sigmund Freud's daughter – 1895–1982), and refers to the

defence mechanism whereby one combats **anxiety** when faced
with authority or a more powerful antagonist by assuming that
person's qualities and attributes. This behaviour is most typical
of children before they have developed capacities for self-
criticism.

## identity crisis

An acute loss of a sense of identity. Identity in human beings
can be equated with a person's essential self that he or she
recognizes as an individual with particular characteristics and
roles, and sees as having a continuous existence over time.
Adolescents quite often experience identity crises as a part of
growing up, when they are still unsure of their social role and
confused over their **self-image**.

## idiot savant /ɪdɪət sævnt/ *or* /idjoʊ sɑːvã/

French, 'learnèd/knowledgeable idiot': a person who has very
limited mental capacities, often being mentally ill or handicapped to the point of needing to be institutionalized, but who
nonetheless has an outstanding talent in one area. This ability is
often for mental arithmetic or for remembering dates and facts.
The incongruity and oddness of this phenomenon gives it great
popular appeal, which has been exploited in the films *Rain Man*,
about an autistic idiot savant, and *Malcolm*, about a mildly
retarded young man with a mechanical genius. However, the
phenomenon is very rare, and its nature is still not understood.

## illusion

A misinterpretation of a perceptual experience. Illusions are
different from **hallucinations** and **delusions** in that they do not
arise from mistaken beliefs, but relate to stimuli that are
actually and objectively present, and their cause is physical
and not psychological. The well-known optical illusions are
experienced in the same way by many different observers. For
these reasons illusions are not of interest to **psychiatrists** or
**psychotherapists**, but are studied mainly by those concerned
with the psychology of perception.

## imago /ɪˈmeɪgoʊ/

In **psychoanalysis**, an **unconscious** and often idealized representation of another person; from Latin, 'image'. The imago is

usually formed in very early life. It is usually that of a parent, and persists into adult life where it influences emotional involvements and relationships.

## implosion

Literally, a bursting or collapsing inward; used in **Laingian** theory to describe a particular kind of fear of loss of identity experienced by people lacking in security about their existence. These individuals feel themselves to be like vacuums, and have a terror of the impingement of reality, fearing that the world will come crashing into their emptiness and obliterate all identity. They withdraw from reality because, although in one way they long for the vacuum to be filled, fear of the annihilation of their fragile identity presents a greater threat.

## implosion therapy

Implosion therapy involves flooding a patient with a particular experience, in order to produce either aversion or **habituation**; also known as **flooding**. In therapy designed to cure antisocial or unhealthy habits, patients are made to indulge in the habit (eg smoking) until they are nauseated by it and lose the desire for it. The second use of the therapy is usually as a treatment for **phobias**, and is like a more extreme form of **desensitization**. Patients are made to confront the situation that provokes phobia, either in reality or in imagination, until they become used to it. The theory is that initially the patient's **anxiety** will rise to its highest level, after which it can only start to drop.

## imprinting

See **sensitive period**

## impulse-control disorders

Disorders marked by the individual's inability to control a need to indulge in some particular antisocial act. Examples of such disorders are **kleptomania, pyromania**, and disorders that are characterized by outbursts of violent behaviour towards people or property.

## inappropriate affect

An emotional response that is, by most people's standards, wholly inappropriate to the situation. A common example is

that of laughing in a very serious or sad situation. Inappropriate affect is one of the indicators of severe psychiatric illness.
See also **affect**

## incidental learning

Learning that takes place without any effort or intention on the part of the learner and without any other party attempting to teach. An example might be learning the words of a pop song that is frequently played in public places, despite the fact that one dislikes the song and makes no conscious attempt to listen to it.

## individual psychology

A term used to describe **Adlerian** psychological theory. By extension it is used of any psychological theory that centres on the striving of the individual's personality as the main force in human development. It is also sometimes used to mean *differential psychology* or the study of *individual differences* – the study of those differences in personality, physiology, learning processes, etc which result in individuals differing from each other in behaviour and performance.

## industrial psychology

A branch of **applied psychology** that applies psychological theory and method to all aspects of the world of work. It covers such aspects as the selection and training of personnel, the workplace environment and its effect on workers, industrial relations, personal interaction between workers, and ergonomics. Increasingly the emphasis has been directed towards the psychology of the organization and organizational dynamics. Partly because of this, and partly because *industrial* is too limited for a field that extends to educational establishments, the armed forces, public services, etc the preferred term now tends to be *organizational psychology*.

## infantile amnesia

Not **amnesia** in infancy, but a term referring to the inability to recall the experiences of early childhood. It is used mainly in **psychoanalysis**, where the phenomenon is regarded as the result of the **repression** of memories of **infantile sexuality** which then extends to all memories of early childhood. Outside the psychoanalytic tradition, psychologists are more inclined to regard infantile amnesia as related to young children's failure to encode events in their memory because they have not yet acquired the necessary language abilities.

## infantile sexuality

A central aspect of **Freudian** theory: the capacity for sexual experience and desire that is assumed to be universal and normal in all young children. In classic Freudian theory this embraces the child's experiences through the **oral** and **anal stages**, and on to the early **genital** or **phallic stage**. Many later **psychoanalytic** theorists have rejected the idea that the pleasure which young children appear to derive from such behaviour as touching or being touched in the genital area is sexual in the way it would be in adults, preferring to regard it as a sensual pleasure.

## inferiority complex

A term in **Adlerian** psychology that has been much taken up in popular use. Adler was originally struck by the way people with physical defects were apparently stimulated to compensate for their organic inferiority. He then formulated the theory that feelings of inferiority and inadequacy – wholly or partly **unconscious** – are an almost universal human experience. Such feelings arise as a reaction to physical defect, inferior physique, parental neglect or ill-treatment, or just to being a small and powerless child, and the individual personality develops according to the strategies adopted to cope with these feelings. The main motivating force in human development becomes **compensation** for inferiority and the striving for superiority, and the mature adult is one who has successfully compensated for his or her feelings of inferiority. Those who have not successfully compensated might either overcompensate and become aggressive or antisocial, or else retreat into illness and **neurosis**. In popular use, anyone who has low **self-esteem** or any small but overbearing person is likely to be described as having an inferiority complex.

## information processing

In **cognitive psychology**, the mental processes involved in organizing, interpreting, and responding to the input of ideas, facts, images, etc that are constantly being presented. The model of computer technology is used as a metaphor for the systematic step-by-step procedures by which people code and decode, store and retrieve information, and is applied to various aspects of the cognitive process, such as memory, decision making, and problem solving.

## inhibition

A term used in several different ways in psychology, but all with the basic idea of the restraining or prevention of a process because of the operation of some external or internal influence. It is used for situations where some basic **emotion** or **drive** blocks another (eg appetite is inhibited by the presence of fear). It is used by learning theorists for the prevention or reduction of a response because of the interference of some other process. In **cognitive psychology** it refers to the reduction in performance, particularly with regard to memory, caused by the presence of other information. In **psychoanalysis**, inhibition refers to the action of the **superego** in controlling the instinctive impulses and desires arising from the **id**. With inhibition, unlike **repression**, the impulse is actually blocked and never reaches the **conscious**.
See also **aim-inhibition**

## inkblot test

Any of the projective tests in **clinical psychology** that use inkblots in order to gain insight into the subject's personality and for purposes of clinical diagnosis. The best known of these tests is the Rorschach (/'rɔːʃɑːk/) test, designed by the Swiss psychiatrist Hermann Rorschach (1844–1922). Subjects are presented with 10 standardized inkblots, some black or grey and some coloured, and asked to describe freely what they see in them. Responses are scored according to a complex standardized system, and interpreted as giving indications of personality traits, neurotic tendencies, etc. Many psychologists are sceptical about the validity and reliability of these tests.

## insanity

Not being sane, suffering from some serious psychiatric disorder. The term is not used as a description or diagnostic term in psychiatry or psychotherapy, and its only remaining use is in the field of law. People cannot be convicted of a crime if they are declared 'insane', ie having a mental disorder or defect which relieves them of criminal responsibility.

See also **McNaghten rules**

## insight learning

Particularly in **Gestalt psychology**, a form of problem solving in which there is an insight into the problem, gained by the sudden reorganization of its elements. This might involve the moment in a practical problem when all its disparate parts suddenly form themselves into a pattern and the solution becomes clear (sometimes called the *aha reaction*). Or it can relate to a **breakthrough** in **psychotherapy**, when the client suddenly sees a significance in the pattern of past events and relationships which leads to self-knowledge and a solution to personal problems.

## instinct

Particularly in animal psychology, an unlearned innate tendency to respond in a particular way that results in a set of fixed and unchanging actions or behaviour patterns characteristic of and universal to a particular species. When used of human beings the term is more likely to be used in the sense of an innate tendency that acts as the motivating force for behaviour. This sense originates in **Freudian** theory. Freud changed his theory on instincts over the years, but always maintained that there was a dualism or polarity between two sets of instincts, and that this led to conflict. His final position postulated two basic instincts, the **death instinct** and the **life instinct**.

## institutionalization

The process of having an individual placed in an institution, such as a mental hospital, prison, or old people's home. It is more often used to describe the process by which people who have been placed in an institution become so used to conforming to the daily rituals, rules, and regulations of the place that they become incapable of living autonomously outside the institution.

## instrumental conditioning
See **operant conditioning**

## intellectualization

The process of treating situations and problems in abstract, logical terms, not involving the **emotions**. In **psychoanalysis** it is regarded as a **defence mechanism**, particularly on the part of people in analysis who want to talk about their problems in a generalized and rational way, and resist the analyst's attempts to put them **in touch** with their emotions and **fantasies**, eg through **free association**. Sometimes patients are very willing to discuss their dreams, memories, and so on, but they seek to control the situation by offering their own carefully worked-out interpretations. Such patients are attempting to control their conflicts and neutralize their emotions by using an intellectual approach to them, feeling threatened by the thought of laying their emotions open to the intrusions of their own **unconscious** or the analyst's interpretations.

## intelligence

Psychologists have been debating the meaning of this concept and developing new theories about it for over 100 years. It is one of the principal areas of conflict in the **nature-nurture controversy**, although most psychologists now would agree that heredity limits intelligence to some extent. Intelligence suggests capacity for cognitive processes such as abstract thinking, reasoning, using judgement and insight, and, perhaps above all, learning from experience and using that learning to deal with new situations. Some would say, cynically, that there can be no satisfactory definition of intelligence, except to say that it is whatever is measured by **intelligence tests**.

## intelligence quotient
See **IQ**

## intelligence test

Any test designed to measure **intelligence**, thought of in terms of ability in abstract reasoning, problem solving, dealing with new situations, etc. Such tests generally contain a number of graded tasks which individuals have to tackle either verbally or in a pencil-and-paper format. Some, but not all, measure **IQ**, and their principal use is as a diagnostic device to predict success in educational and occupational contexts.

There are many problems surrounding intelligence testing. They are designed by psychologists who are usually white, middle-class, urban individuals who conceive of successful cognitive ability as functioning within a culture similar to their own. It is likely, therefore, that most intelligence tests have a built-in sociocultural bias. Their reliability is also called into question by the beliefs that coaching and practice can improve scores on tests, while **anxiety** and poor **motivation** can affect scores adversely. Other questions arise from the difficulties associated wtih defining intelligence. Is intelligence something that can be measured? Can intelligence tests measure creativity or original thinking? Does a high score on an intelligence test indicate anything other than that the individual is good at performing on intelligence tests?

See also **Binet Scale; culture-free tests; Stanford-Binet Scale; Wechsler Scales**

### internalization

A term which usually refers to the way people come to accept external beliefs, **attitudes**, standards of behaviour, etc as their own. In **psychoanalytic** theory, the emergence of the **superego** is the result of the **unconscious** process by which individuals internalize the values and principles of their parents, making them part of their own mental apparatus. This process is sometimes called *introjection*. In **social psychology**, internalization is the opposite of **externalization**, and relates to attributing one's behaviour to internal **motivation** rather than external forces. The term is also sometimes used to mean having very thoroughly learned some complex system, such as the grammar of a language.

### intolerance of ambiguity

See **tolerance of ambiguity**

### in touch

Not a technical term, but one used a great deal by **psychotherapists** and **counsellors**. It is often thought to be one of the main aims of therapy to put clients 'in touch with their emotions', particularly when they have been using **intellec-**

**tualization** or other **defence mechanisms** to try to avoid facing them. When therapists talk of being 'in touch with one's anger', for example, they mean acknowledging that the anger exists, examining the experience of feeling anger, and realizing who it is directed at, how it makes one feel, etc. *In touch* is also sometimes used in terms of **empathy** with other people's emotions, as in 'an ability to get in touch with other people's pain'.

## introjection

See **internalization**

## introvert

A term in popular use, but deriving from **Jungian** personality theory. It literally means 'turned inward', from Latin *intro* 'inward' + *vertere* 'to turn'. According to Jungian theory, an introvert is someone who is characterized by being preoccupied by his or her own mental life, unsociable, withdrawn, and preferring reflection to activity. Introverts are shy, wary in making new relationships, and dislike new social situations and large social gatherings. The introverted personality can be thoughtful, sensitive, and imaginative, but in extreme form can be passive and inward-looking to the point of being incapable of forming relationships. For objections to the polar theory of introversion/extraversion, see **extravert**.

## IQ

An abbreviation of **intelligence quotient**. It is a score representing **intelligence**, and is derived by dividing an individual's *mental age* (as measured by performance on a standardized **intelligence test**) by his or her actual or *chronological age*, and multiplying the result by 100. On this basis, an average IQ is 100, about half the population would have IQs between 90 and 110, 25 per cent would be above this range and 25 per cent below. An IQ of above about 140 is considered a sign that a person is exceptionally gifted intellectually, and an IQ below about 70 indicates **mental retardation**.
See also **Binet Scale; Stanford-Binet Scale; Wechsler Scales**

## isolation

In **psychoanalysis**, a **defence mechanism** whereby people unconsciously isolate an occurrence or event to prevent it from connecting up to the rest of their experience. They do not actually forget the event in question, but keep it separated from the **emotions** and **impulses** that it is connected with, and refuse to recognize it as a memory source. Isolation is sometimes associated with using formulas and rituals, and it is thought to be particularly characteristic of **obsessive-compulsive disorders**.

# J

## jealousy

An emotional state involving **anxiety** in relation to a loved object, where there is insecurity about that person's reciprocal love. Jealousy is different from **envy** in that it always involves a third party, who is regarded as a rival for the affections of the loved one. Jealousy can become pathological and lead to **delusions** and **paranoia**. For **Freudian** theorists, jealousy is linked to the **Oedipus complex**.

## Jungian /ˈjʊŋiən/

Relating to the theories of Carl Gustav Jung (1857–1961), Swiss psychiatrist and psychoanalyst. He was one of Freud's early colleagues, but broke away from **Freudian psychoanalytic** theory because he could not agree with Freud's insistence on the importance of **infantile sexuality** as the basis of **neurosis**. Jung's theory is more inclined to religion and mysticism, and is based on the idea of the **collective unconscious** and its **archetypes**, and the interpretation of universal **symbols** in dreams, myth, and art. The other most significant aspect of Jungian thought is in the area of **personality** theory, to which he contributed the idea of the **extravert** and **introvert**. Jungian theory is also sometimes known as *analytic psychology*.

See also **anima; animus; Electra complex; mandala; persona**

# K

## Kleinian

Relating to the theories of the Austrian **psychoanalyst** Melanie Klein (1882–1960), who was a pioneer in the use of psychoanalysis with children. Her views differ from classical **Freudian** theory in several respects. The primary difference is Klein's belief that the origins of **neurosis** start in the first year of life, and are based not on **fixation** at a certain stage of psychosexual development, but on failure to pass through a *depressive position* caused by ambivalence towards the mother and her breast.

See also **death instinct; envy; idealization; reparation; splitting**

## kleptomania

An **impulse-control disorder** characterized by being unable to resist the temptation to steal; from Greek *klepto* 'to steal' + *mania*. Typically kleptomaniacs have no economic need to steal, and usually steal things that are useless to them rather than items they really want or need.

# L

## labelling

Particularly in **educational psychology**, attaching a simplistic diagnostic term to individuals or groups to describe a condition or problem which is almost certainly more complex and diverse than the 'label' suggests, and which may have connotations of stigma. An example of such a label is **mental retardation**. The term *labelling theory* is used, particularly in **social psychology** and by critics of **psychiatry**, to describe the way in which people who exhibit deviant or unacceptable behaviour are labelled as 'psychotic', 'paranoid', or whatever. This results in a **self-fulfilling prophecy**, as once people have been labelled with a standard psychiatric diagnostic term, they will be regarded by professionals, family, and eventually themselves, in accordance with that label, and all their behaviour will be interpreted in its light and seen as confirmation of the diagnosis.

## Laingian /ˈlæŋiən/

Relating to the theories of R D Laing (1927–89), Scottish psychiatrist and psychoanalyst and exponent of **existential psychology** and **existential therapy**. He is influential particularly through his existential analysis of **alienation**, and his work on **schizophrenia** and its origins in family relationships.
See also **engulfment; implosion; petrification**

## latency period

In **psychoanalysis**, the period between about 5 years old and the onset of adolescence. This stage marks the end of **infantile sexuality** and the dissolution of the **Oedipus complex**; sexual interest is apparently absent or **sublimated** until it reappears at puberty. One of the problems with this theory is that it cannot be regarded as universal, as it does not hold for cultures where sexual activity in prepubescent children is seen as normal.

## latent content

In **dream analysis** the 'real' meaning of the dream that is revealed in its interpretation. This meaning is hidden through

75

the dreamer's **repression** and **censorship**, which cause the dream to be presented in a coded form. Revealing the latent content of a dream involves decoding or translating a narrative or series of images into the unconscious thoughts and wishes that they represent.

See also **manifest content**

## lateral thinking

Literally, 'thinking coming from the side'. The term was coined by the Maltese-born psychologist Edward de Bono (1933– ) for a method of problem solving where, instead of using the direct and obvious approach, one looks at the problem from new angles and reaches a creative solution.

## learned helplessness

A theory of human **motivation** which suggests that the feeling of helplessness and being unable to control one's situation is learned by past experiences of failure. The theory was based on animal experiments where dogs were given electric shocks in a situation where it was impossible to escape. Eventually they became so passive that they did not avoid the shocks even when an avenue of escape was made available. The human version of this phenomenon is when repeated failure results in people feeling that there is no connection between their behaviour and what happens to them, and they cease to make any efforts to avoid negative outcomes. The term is often used in **educational psychology** of children who are used to academic failure and who have come to believe that there is no way that they can improve their situation by their own effort. Such children have low **self-esteem**, have no motivation to learn, and often suffer from **anxiety** and **depression**. They have an external **locus of control**, attributing academic success or failure to causes such as luck, the whims of teachers, and so on.

## learning disability

A diagnostic term in **educational psychology**, covering a wide range of disorders in which there is difficulty with learning, for example, to use language and communcation skills, read, write, spell, or do mathematics. Children are usually classifed as learning disabled when there is a severe discrepancy between their **ability** (as measured on a standardized **intelligence test**) and their intellectual achievement.

### lesbianism
See **homosexuality**

### leucotomy
See **lobotomy**

### libido /lɪˈbiːdoʊ/
Latin, 'desire'. In popular use it refers simply to lust or sexual desire, but its origins in **psychoanalysis** are more complex. In early **Freudian** theory it denoted the energy that accompanied the sexual **drive**. Freud later modified this idea so that the libido was not exclusively sexual, but was a more generalized form of life energy or psychic energy that accompanied all strong desires or drives, and Jung also used the term in this sense. However, it is still usually used in Freud's earlier sense.
See also **Eros; life instinct**

### lie detector
An instrument that measures physiological changes such as pulse rate, respiration, galvanic skin response, and blood pressure in subjects while they are being questioned. The theory is that, if they tell lies, they will experience emotional **stress** and **anxiety**, and will show the physiological changes associated with that emotional state. Although lie detectors have been used in police interrogations since the 1920s, and are still sometimes used, most psychologists are sceptical about their reliability. Some people feel little or no guilt and/or do not believe in the lie detector's efficiency, so are not made anxious by the fact that they are lying. Other innocent people may be made very anxious by a question for reasons that are quite irrelevant to what the investigation is about, and may show all the physiological symptoms of acute stress.

### life instinct
A **Freudian** term for all the **drives** that are aimed at the preservation of life, as opposed to the self-destructive **death instinct**. The life instinct is part of later Freudian theory, and is linked with his final version of the **libido**, which is the energy that is attached to all the aspects of the life instinct: sexuality, creativity, and the desire for unity.
See also **Eros**

## Likert scale

Technique used in **attitude testing**, invented by the American social psychologist Rensis Likert (1903–). Respondents are given a series of statements expressing attitudes, and asked to rate them according to how far they agree or disagree with them. The usual Likert scale is a five-point scale – 'strongly agree', 'agree', 'uncertain', 'disagree', 'strongly disagree' – although three-point and seven-point scales are sometimes used.

## limen

See **threshold**

## Little Albert

An 11-month-old boy used in an experiment by the American **behaviourist** psychologist J B Watson (1878–1958). In order to prove his theory that basic emotions, such as fear, are a result of **conditioning**, Watson created a fear of rats and other furry things in Albert by showing him a white rat at the same time as making a loud noise.

## Little Hans

The pseudonym used by Freud for a 5-year-old boy in one of his most famous case histories, published in 1909. Little Hans had a **phobia** about horses, which Freud interpreted as being related to his **Oedipus** and **castration complexes**. Although the case of Little Hans is spoken of as the first psychoanalysis of a young child, Freud only actually met Hans once, and the analysis was conducted by the child's father (who had undergone analysis himself), under Freud's direction. It was not until the 1930s, with the work of Anna Freud and Melanie Klein, that young children were psychoanalysed without involving their parents.

## lobotomy

A surgical procedure aimed at curing severe psychological disorders; also known as **leucotomy, prefrontal lobotomy,** or **psychosurgery**. It involves severing the nerve fibres between the frontal lobes of the brain and the region containing the thalamus and hypothalamus. It was first carried out in the 1930s, but is now rarely performed, as its negative side-effects – apathy, deterioration in intellect, insensitivity to others – are irreversible, and its beneficial effects can generally be produced by tranquillizing drugs.

## locus of control

In **personality** theory, an individual's perception of the source of control over events and experiences. People with an *internal* locus of control believe that events are largely determined by their own behaviour, that they are responsible for their actions, and that they can control what happens to them. People with an *external* locus see control as coming from outside forces or other people rather than from their own behaviour. They often attribute their success or failure in life to fate or luck, and have little **motivation** to pursue personal achievement.

## long-term memory

Both the process of recalling information after a relatively long time, and the actual memory itself; sometimes also called **long-term store**. Long-term memory is the permanent store for information that has been processed and interpreted, and although it can contain a huge volume of material it is subject to deterioration.

# M

## Machiavellianism /mækiəˈvɛliənɪzm/

A **personality** characteristic or behaviour pattern which involves manipulating other people for one's own personal advantage, opportunism, and using devious methods to increase one's own power. The word comes from the cynical political views of the Italian writer and statesman Niccolò Machiavelli (1469–1527). A *Machiavellian scale* (or *Mach Scale*) has been designed to measure subjects' degree of Machiavellianism, according to their rating of statements, some of which are actually taken straight from Machiavelli's writings.

## magical thinking

The belief that there is a connection between what one thinks or wishes and what happens in the world. It is typical in cultures based on magic and animism, and is normal in young children. At a certain stage of development, most children believe that if they wish for something hard enough they can make it happen, and would also feel responsible if for example they have hoped that something unpleasant would happen to a sibling and then it does. In adults in developed Western cultures, this kind of thinking is thought to be a sign of alienation from reality and symptomatic of psychological disturbance, although in fact many 'normal' adults can sometimes find themselves thinking in this way.

## mandala /mænˈdɑːlə/

A magical circle represented in a picture or diagram with symbolic figures, symmetrically arranged and radiating around a central point; from Sanskrit, 'circle'. It is found in Buddhism and Tantric Hinduism where it symbolizes the nature of the deity and is used in worship and meditation. It is an important term in **Jungian** theory. Jung found mandalas or mandala-like symbolism occurring spontaneously in the dreams and drawings of some of his patients, and interpreted this as part of the process of integrating **unconscious** material by the **conscious** to create a unified individual self. Although it is a religious symbol, the mandala usually occurs in the dreams and visions of those who do not believe, or have ceased believing, in an external God.

## mania

Literally 'madness', from Greek *mainesthai* 'to be mad'. It is used as a suffix in such terms as **megalomania** to denote a particular form of mental disturbance, and in **kleptomania, nymphomania, pyromania**, etc to denote uncontrollable urges towards particular kinds of behaviour. The term principally, however, denotes an abnormal state characterized by extreme excitement and activity, often accompanied by a feeling of euphoria and elation. Manic patients usually think and talk very rapidly, jumping from one idea to another but with little rationality or self-criticism; they suffer from insomnia, and eventually become exhausted from overactivity and lack of sleep; they are impulsive, sometimes suffer from **delusions**, and may be violent. Mania is found in various **affective disorders**, but particularly in **manic depression**.

## manic depression

One of the most common **affective disorders**, characterized by cyclical attacks of severe **depression** and of **mania**, usually interspersed with periods of normality, although some patients regularly alternate between manic and depressive episodes. Treatment is usually with *lithium*, an antimania drug, and antidepressants during depressive episodes. The disorder is also known as *bipolar disorder* and *manic-depressive psychosis*.
See also **oral character**

## manifest content

In **dream analysis,** the overt content of a dream that the dreamer remembers and recounts on waking. It can be regarded as the final draft which has passed through the dreamer's **censorship** system, and which needs analysis and interpretation to reveal and decode its hidden meaning.
See also **latent content**

## masochism

The experience of sexual pleasure and satisfaction through experiencing physical pain or humiliation. The word derives from the Austrian novelist Leopold von Sacher-Masoch (1835–

95), who described the phenomenon in his writings. It is most often used in the sexual context, but it is also sometimes used for any tendency to turn hostile or destructive impulses upon oneself, or to alleviate guilt by seeking punishment (including self-punishment).
See also **sadism; sadomasochism**

## mass hysteria

A popular term, but one not used by psychologists or psychiatrists, though it is still to be found in some medical dictionaries. It is most aptly applied to cases where large numbers of people experience false perceptions or suffer the same symptoms of illness, with no physiological cause. There are well-documented cases of outbreaks of mass fainting or vomiting in girls' schools, or mysterious illnesses in workplaces. It could reasonably be claimed that such phenomena exhibit some of the classical symptoms of **hysteria**; they are sometimes referred to as *hysterical contagion*. The term *mass hysteria* is often used to describe the behaviour of people at Nazi rallies or at revivalist religious meetings, but such forms of collective behaviour have no relation to hysteria, and are more relevant to sociologists than psychologists.

## matching

See **mirroring and matching**

## maternal deprivation

Lack of loving care and nurture from a mother or mother substitute in the early years. Maternal deprivation is responsible for symptoms of **anxiety** and physical and emotional retardation in both human and higher mammal species. Most of the research on maternal deprivation was carried out before it was acknowledged that fathers (human ones, at least) were also capable of nurturing and caring for infants, and it might now be more appropriate to speak of *parental deprivation*.
See also **separation anxiety**

## McNaghten rules

A legal ruling formulated by the judges of the House of Lords in 1843 that set a precedent for a defence of **insanity**, and is still widely used in legal systems based on the English model. The rules state that a person cannot be held legally responsible for a crime, if at the time it was committed, he or she was 'labouring under such a deficit of reason from disease of the mind as not to know the nature or quality of the act . . . or did not know that he was doing what was wrong'. In 1957 the law was amended so that anyone on a murder charge whose 'mental responsibility' was substantially impaired by mental illness could plead 'diminished responsibility' and be convicted of manslaughter. The case that gave the rules their name was that of one McNaghten who suffered from **paranoia**. Under the **delusion** that he was being persecuted by Sir Robert Peel, he murdered the statesman's private secretary.

## megalomania
A **personality disorder** characterized by greatly exaggerated evaluation of one's own power, ability, and importance; from Greek *megalo* 'very large' + **mania**. It sometimes includes **delusions** of grandeur, for example the belief that one is an extremely rich, important, and famous person.

## melancholia
A rather outdated term for extreme **depression**, with apathy, suicidal tendencies, and a slowing down of movement and thought processes; sometimes used for the depressive phase of **manic depression**. The word comes from *melancholy*, which derives from Greek 'black bile', and originates in the medieval belief that the composition of 'humours' or bodily fluids (blood, phlegm, yellow bile, and black bile) determined a person's temperament.

## mental handicap
See **mental retardation**

## mental illness
A term covering all forms of disabling psychological problem, emotional impairment, or behavioural disorder severe enough to warrant psychiatric treatment. The term *mental disorder* is now often preferred. It is important to distinguish mental illness or disorder from **mental retardation** or *mental handicap*.

## mental retardation

A general term for all forms of intellectual functioning that is considerably below average; also called *mental handicap*, but to be distinguished from **mental illness**. The cause of mental retardation is generally brain damage or a congenital condition such as *Down's syndrome*. A mentally retarded child is slow at reaching the normal developmental milestones, and cannot be expected ever to achieve normal levels of behavioural and cognitive functioning.

Classification is according to results on standardized **intelligence tests**. Those with **IQ** scores of around 70 to 85 are considered to have **borderline** intelligence and are not classified as mentally retarded. Those with IQs in the 55–69 range – the majority of mentally retarded people – are classified as having *mild mental retardation*; they are able to acquire some academic skills through special education programmes and can achieve some degree of independence living in a community. Those with IQs of 40 to 54 are classified as having *moderate mental retardation* and are capable of learning limited academic skills and being trained in simple communication, self-help, social skills, and vocational skills. Those with IQs below 40 – about 8 per cent of mentally retarded people – have *severe mental retardation*; they are unable to learn academic or vocational skills and need constant supervision and care. The old terminology which related to the concept of *mental deficiency* and which included terms such as *moron*, *imbecile*, and *idiot*, is no longer used.

## milieu therapy /miljɜ:/

Any form of therapy that concentrates on helping people by changing or modifying their immediate environment or life circumstances. This usually means placing people in some kind of **therapeutic community** with a controlled environment.

## Minnesota Multiphasic Personality Inventory (MMPI)

An inventory formulated at the University of Minnesota in the 1940s, and still widely used as a test of **personality** characteristics and as a diagnostic tool in **clinical psychology**. It is a paper-and-pencil test in which subjects are presented with a series of 550 statements about feelings and behaviour, and asked to mark each one 'true', 'false', or 'cannot say'. Analysis of the answers yields scores relating to such disorders as **depression, hysteria, schizophrenia, compulsions**, and **phobias**, and personality factors such as degree of **anxiety**, masculinity-feminity, and **locus of control**.

## mirroring and matching

Techniques used in **counselling**, designed to establish rapport and show **empathy** with the client. In mirroring, the counsellor produces exactly the same behaviour as the client, eg adopting the same tone of voice, using the same form of words, taking up the same bodily posture, or sighing or smiling when the client does. Matching is similar, but the counsellor produces some approximation to the client's behaviour rather than mirroring it exactly, eg moving a hand to the rhythm of the client's speech. These techniques are supposed to be performed subtly, and not to be apparent or obvious to the client.

## modelling

In **social psychology**, the process of observing another person or group of people who are thought of as being desirable and worthy of imitation, and adopting the same characteristics and forms of behaviour as the model or models. It differs from **psychoanalytic** ideas such as **identification** in that the modelling is always **conscious**, and the chosen role model may well be someone with whom the person has no close emotional bonds. Modelling is regarded as a learning process and thought to be one of the main ways in which **socialization** takes place.

## moral development

An area of **developmental psychology** concerned with the development of moral reasoning and the ability to make moral judgements. One of the most important theories of moral development is the **developmental stage** theory formulated by American psychologist Lawrence Kohlberg (1927–), working on **Piagetian** principles. According to this theory children gradually progress from simply avoiding punishment to seeking approval, and finally to developing personal principles and conscience and a concern for community values. In **social-learning theory** the development of morality is mainly a matter of observation of acceptable and unacceptable moral behaviour with its concomitant rewards and punishments, and **modelling** oneself on those whose behaviour is acceptable. In

**psychoanalysis** moral development is part of the process of **identification** and **internalization**.

## motivation

In general, the process or state that impels individuals to action. It is closely related to the idea of **drives** and needs, and behaviour directed towards satisfying or achieving aims or goals. There are many psychological theories of motivation, but they can be roughly divided into the physiological and behavioural, on the one hand, and the social and **psychoanalytic** on the other. The former concentrate on the study of behaviour aimed at satisfying basic human and animal drives, and the learning that accompanies it. The latter are concerned with more complex forms of motivation, shown by human individuals relating to society and its demands, or with unconscious motivation, one of the central theories of psychoanalysis.

## multiple personality

A rare psychiatric disorder, but one that has become well-known to lay people through such popular films as *The Three Faces of Eve*. It is a dissociative disorder (see **dissociation**) in which the integrity of the personality becomes fragmented and two or more distinct subpersonalities emerge. Often these different personalities behave, talk, dress, and write in completely different ways, and usually adopt different names. Sometimes they are unaware of each other; sometimes they are aware, in which case they are often mutually critical and hostile. When there are just two distinct personalities the term *dual personality* is often used. The term *split personality* is also used for the condition, and this often leads to confusion between multiple personality and the much more common disorder **schizophrenia**, which is in no way related to it.

## Munchausen syndrome /ˈmʊntʃaʊzən/

A disorder in which people pretend to have serious physical illnesses and simulate all the appropriate symptoms. They usually seek hospitalization and surgical treatment, often going from one hospital to another, gaining more information about their supposed illness at each hospital so as to better deceive the surgeons at the next one. It is named after Baron Karl von Münchhausen, a legendary teller of tall stories.

# N

## N Ach
See **need for achievement**

## naive subject

In **experimental psychology**, a subject in an experiment who is unfamiliar with experiments or who has not previously been subjected to some particular experimental situation. In this sense it can be used of both human and animal subjects. A further sense, used usually in **social psychology**, is a subject who is not aware of the real purpose of an experiment, or who has been deliberately misled about it, because it would defeat the purpose of the experiment if the subject knew what it was (see **single-blind**). For example, in an experiment to see how people behave when they believe there is a fire, subjects may be told that they are to be given a test of short-term memory, and asked to sit in a room to wait for the experimenter. While they are waiting, a smoke-producing machine introduces smoke into the waiting room and the subjects' reactions are observed.

## narcissism

Excessive love of oneself; from the Greek myth of Narcissus, a beautiful young man who fell in love with his own reflection. It is used with different emphases in **psychiatry** and **psychoanalysis**. In the former, narcissism is classed as a **personality disorder** characterized by an exaggerated regard for oneself and an overestimation of one's appearance and abilities, an excessive need for admiration and hostility towards criticism, and an apparent inability to direct love towards others. In classic psychoanalytic theory, narcissism is a continuation into adult life of the early stage of psychosexual development when the **libido** is directed towards the self. Such adults often prefer auto-erotism or masturbation to a sexual relationship with another person. When they are able to love anyone other than themselves, their choice will be directed towards someone with very similar looks or characteristics to themselves.

## narcoanalysis

**Psychotherapy** carried out while the patient is in a sleep-like state under the influence of drugs, usually barbiturates; from Greek *narkē* 'numbness, torpor'. The idea is that the patient's defences will be down and he or she will be more open to accepting the analyst's interpretations. The process is also called *narcotherapy*, particularly when the psychotherapy is not psychoanalytically oriented.

## narcolepsy

A condition characterized by recurrent and uncontrollable spells of deep sleep during the day; from the Greek *narkē* 'numbness, torpor' + *lépsis* 'seizure'. The causes of narcolepsy are not known, but treatment is generally with stimulant drugs.

## nature-nurture controversy

The long-standing debate among psychologists as to whether behaviour patterns, intelligence, personality, etc are influenced more by genetic and hereditary factors or by learning and environment; often called the **heredity-environment contro-versy**. There have been times when the controversy has been very heated, particularly in the area of **intelligence**, where it has sometimes seemed that political sympathies were encroaching on academic objectivity. Those who insisted that intelligence was genetically influenced and a matter of heredity were often accused of racism, while those who believed that any child could achieve a high standard of intellectual performance if its upbringing and teaching were favourable were accused of mindless egalitarianism. It is now generally believed that genetic background does produce some limitations on ability and other characteristics, but that within these limitations environmental factors can produce important differences.
See also **twin studies**

## need for achievement (N Ach)

A term associated particularly with the work of the American psychologist David McClelland (1917– ). It relates to the strong motivation to achieve excellence and to succeed in competitive fields. The trait can be measured by **projective techniques**.

## need for affiliation

A term in **social psychology** invented by the American psychologist Henry A. Murray (1893–1988), to describe the need to be with other people. This applies to a need for social intercourse, friendship, and a feeling of belonging, and to the need to have others sharing one's experiences, even when they are unpleasant.

## negative reinforcement

In **conditioning**, training a response through the use of an aversive stimulus, such as an electric shock. It differs from punishment, in that with negative reinforcement a desired response is made more likely or more frequent by the removal of the aversive stimulus (eg rats are trained to press a lever by giving them an electric shock, the shock being stopped when they press the lever), whereas in punishment the aversive stimulus follows undesirable behaviour (eg rats are trained to avoid pressing a lever by giving them an electric shock when they touch the lever). However, outside the strict context of conditioning, the term negative reinforcement is quite often used synonymously with punishment.

## negative transfer

The phenomenon whereby skills and knowledge acquired in learning a particular task have a detrimental effect on learning a subsequent task. For example, it is harder to learn the use of the acute accent in Italian if you have already learned the quite different way that it is used in French.

## neo-Freudian

All **psychoanalytic** theorists have been influenced by Freud, to a greater or lesser extent. However, *neo-Freudian* (the prefix *neo* is from Greek 'new') is, strictly speaking, restricted to one particular group of analysts practising in the USA, and to their followers. This group, whose best-known members were the German-born psychoanalysts Erich Fromm (1900–80) and Karen Horney (1885–1952), and the American Harry Stack Sullivan (1892–1949), reinterpreted Freudian theory with new emphasis on social and cultural aspects of personality development and less stress on biological instincts.

## nervous breakdown

A popular and non-technical term, not used by professionals in **psychology** and **psychiatry**. It is generally used to describe a disabling attack of emotional disturbance, often severe enough to require hospital treatment. The kind of mental illness involved is usually a **neurotic** rather than a **psychotic** disorder.

## neurasthenia

An obsolescent term for a state of debility originally thought to have nervous origins, from Greek *neuro* 'pertaining to the nerves' + *astheneia* 'weakness'. It is characterized by extreme fatigue and physical weakness, often accompanied by lack of motivation, depressive symptoms and physical symptoms such as headache and insomnia. Patients with such symptoms are now likely to be diagnosed as suffering from a physical – possibly viral – disease, from mild **depression**, or from a **psychosomatic disorder**.

## neurosis

A psychological disturbance with no organic cause, although it was originally thought to arise from a disorder of the nervous system; from Greek *neuro* 'pertaining to the nerves' + *-osis* 'abnormal condition'. The modern use of the term began with Freud, who subdivided neuroses into several subtypes, including **anxiety** neurosis, **hysteria, phobic** neurosis, and **obsessive-compulsive** neurosis. According to classical **Freudian** theory, all neuroses have their roots in emotional conflicts in childhood. The term is no longer used diagnostically by **psychiatrists**, who have largely replaced it with *neurotic disorder*. Like neurosis, this denotes a mental condition which has no organic cause, but it is neutral as to the actual cause or origin. Neurosis has traditionally been contrasted with **psychosis**, and the same distinctions can be made between the current terms of neurotic and **psychotic disorders**. A neurotic disorder, while distressing and debilitating, does not involve the severe loss of contact with reality found in psychotic disorders, and is more amenable to **psychotherapy**,

## neurotic disorder

See **neurosis**

## non-directive counselling

A form of **counselling** in which the counsellor concentrates on showing **empathy** with clients; has no preconceived interpretations of their problems; does not give direct advice; and does not evaluate or guide what clients say, but helps them to clarify their thoughts in order to facilitate them to solve their own problems. It is closely related to **client-centred therapy**, and is based on the theories of the American psychologist Carl Rogers (1902–87).

## non-directive therapy

See **client-centred therapy**

## non-verbal tests

See **performance tests**

## nymphomania

Excessive sexual desire in women; from Latin *nymphae*, a term for the *labia minora* or inner lips of the vulva, + **mania**. Although the term is often popularly applied to any woman who is extremely enthusiastic about sex and has a great many sexual partners, true nymphomania is a rare condition in which satisfaction is never achieved and enjoyment is irrelevant. It is generally regarded as a symptom of a severe psychological disorder.

See also **satyriasis**

# O

## object

A term used in quite different ways in psychology and **psychoanalysis**. In psychological theory connected with perception and cognition, an object is an aspect of the environment that a perceiving subject is aware of. The word is also sometimes used as a synonym for the noun *objective* in its meaning of a goal or aim.

In psychoanalytic theory an object is that towards which actions, thoughts, and desires are directed. It can be the thing or person through which the instinct seeks to attain its aim, or the thing or person towards which emotions are directed. The object is nearly always a person or a part of a person (eg the mother's breast) or a symbol of one of these. Many psychoanalytical terms contain the word: these include *object choice* (the selection of someone as a love object); *bad object* and *good object* (an internal or external object of hatred or love); *object loss* (loss of a loved object or loss of the love for that object); and *transitional object* (an object which a child treats as being somewhere between itself and another person, typically a doll, soft toy, or bit of cloth used as a comforter).

See also **object relations theory**


## object relations theory

A **psychoanalytic** theory which concentrates on people's relationships with **objects** outside of the self. Although the stress is usually on **fantasy** about the objects and the relationships, rather than about real factual relationships, the theory departs from classical **Freudian** theory in shifting away from the idea of **instinct** as being central to the explanation of **personality** and **motivation**.


## obsession

Thoughts or ideas which persistently intrude upon someone's **conscious** mind, against the person's will and despite the person realizing that the idea is abnormal or inappropriate. It differs from **compulsion** in centring on thought rather than behaviour, but the two often go hand-in-hand (see **obsessive-compulsive disorder**).

## obsessive-compulsive disorder

A disorder characterized by obsessive thoughts and compulsive behaviour; formerly known as **obsessional neurosis**. Typically a person suffering from such a disorder has a personality similar to the traditional **anal character**: inflexible, inhibited, overconscientious, and plagued by feelings of doubt and **anxiety** about losing control. The obsessive thoughts generally suggest the compulsive action, and the patient reaches an unbearable state of anxiety which is only satisfied by acting on the compulsion. The compulsive behaviour is usually very ritualistic, and often involves washing the hands or other objects, counting or touching things, or repeating words or phrases. There is often an obsession with germs or dirt, where patients are compelled to wash everything that they or anyone else uses during the day, such as washing the door-handle after anyone has come in or out of a room. Often a patient's life, and their family's, can be totally disrupted by their need to perform these time-consuming and complicated rituals. In the **psychoanalytic** tradition the condition is linked to fixation at the **anal stage**, or to a high degree of **internalization**, and is treated by **psychoanalysis**. Other forms of **psychotherapy**, and **hypnosis**, have been used with such patients; but most are treated by some form of **behaviour modification**.

## occupational therapy

The use of purposeful activity to occupy patients with physical or psychiatric disorders, usually in a hospital setting. The therapy is designed to aid recovery and rehabilitation by restoring patients' feelings of **self-esteem**, promoting vocational skills, providing an outlet for creative abilities, etc. Some hospitals for long-term mentally ill or mentally handicapped patients have workshops where patients are daily employed in simple craft or light industrial work, and many have units where daily living skills such as cooking can be practised to aid the patients' return to the community.

## Oedipal stage

See **genital stage**

## Oedipus complex

A collection, or **complex**, of **unconscious** wishes, both loving and hostile, experienced by a child in its feelings towards its parents. In classical **Freudian** theory, it arises in the child between 3 and 5 years of age, and involves love and sexual desire for the parent of the opposite sex, together with feelings of jealous rivalry and a desire to eliminate the parent of the same sex. The term comes from the mythical Greek king Oedipus who (unwittingly) killed his father and married his mother. Freud took the complex to be a universal phenomenon, resolved only by a mature **identification** with the same-sex parent and a satisfactory sexual relationship with a person of the opposite sex. Most **psychoanalysts** since Freud have modified the theory somewhat; few have totally rejected it, but many theorists do not believe it to be universal.

See also **Electra complex**

## operant conditioning

A form of **conditioning** in which learning takes place when **reinforcement** follows a person's or animal's spontaneous response; also known as **instrumental conditioning**. For example, a rat exploring its cage might press a lever, and find that a food pellet appears. It will then learn to press the lever in order to obtain food.

See also **Skinnerian**

## oral character

In **psychoanalysis**, someone who is **fixated** at the **oral stage** of psychosexual development. People who are orally fixated derive pleasure from oral activity such as thumb-sucking, eating and drinking, smoking, and even excessive talking. Personality traits typical of the oral character are, on the one hand, optimism, generosity, elation, and dependence; on the other, pessimism, **depression**, and aggression. The first cluster of traits are thought to be linked to good experiences at the oral stage, the latter with bad experiences and early weaning. However, it is common for both sets of traits to be present in the same person, and some psychoanalytic theorists associate the mood swings of **manic depression** with the oral character.

## oral stage

In **psychoanalysis**, the first stage of psychosexual development, during the first year of life, where erotic pleasure is derived from the sensations associated with feeding. The German psychoanalyst Karl Abraham (1877–1925) elaborated Freud's basic theory, and suggested that the oral stage should be subdivided into an *early oral stage*, where pleasure is derived from sucking, and a later *oral-sadistic stage*, after the child acquires teeth, where pleasure is associated with biting.
See also **oral character**

## organizational psychology

See **industrial psychology**

## orgone theory

A theory invented by the Austrian-born American psychoanalyst Wilhelm Reich (1897–1957). According to Reich, the orgone is a vital life force or kind of energy that pervades all nature and is universally present, but is most intensely present during sexual orgasm. He devised a form of therapy based on this theory, known as *orgonomy* or *orgone therapy*, designed to help the client achieve the orgasmic release which Reich believed was an essential part of the therapeutic process. Although Reich's views on the dangers of repressing children's sexuality were influential, his later writings on orgones and the central importance of the orgasm have never been widely accepted.

## overachievement

Achievement beyond the level that would be predicted. The term is usually used in **educational psychology** for students who perform better on tasks than **intelligence** or **aptitude** tests have indicated that they would perform. It sometimes carries the suggestion that such people are 'trying too hard' and are ambitious for achievement beyond their abilities.
See also **underachievement**

## overcompensation

See **compensation**

## overdetermined

In **psychoanalysis**, the word has several meanings. It is usually applied to dreams or to symptoms of **neurosis**, which are said to be overdetermined if they express more than one **unconscious** drive or conflict. In fact, classical **Freudian** theory holds that virtually all behaviour is overdetermined, and it is the task of the analyst to sort out the many different layers of meaning and causation.

# P

## panic disorders

A type of **anxiety** disorder, characterized by frequent panic attacks with no obvious precipitating cause. A sense of dread, fear, and unreality is often accompanied by physical symptoms such as palpitations and sweating. The word *panic* is derived from the name of the Greek god Pan, whose presence was said to induce sudden irrational terror and flight.

## paranoia

A word deriving from Greek *paranous* 'disorder of the mind', and originally denoting mental illness in general. However, it is now used specifically for a **psychotic disorder** marked by persistent **delusions** of persecution and often intense and irrational jealousy. Less often, there are delusions of grandeur. There are no accompanying **hallucinations**, and sufferers can appear quite intelligent and lucid outside the context of their delusions which they will defend vigorously, refusing to hear any evidence that contradicts them. Paranoiac patients organize their delusions into a system that is internally consistent and coherent, and will act in a way that is rational given the assumptions of their system of delusions.

The adjective *paranoid* is often used to describe conditions that include symptoms of paranoia – such as excessive suspicion, jealousy, belief that one is being plotted against – without necessarily having the specific diagnosed illness of paranoia. Thus a paranoid **personality disorder** is one that exhibits some of these symptoms but without having the thoroughly systematized structure of delusions. Paranoid **schizophrenia** is a form of schizophrenia where delusions of persecution and jealousy are common.

## parapraxis

See **Freudian slip**.

## parapsychology

The branch of psychology that deals with *psychic research* or the

97

investigation of paranormal phenomena. These phenomena can be roughly divided into two groups: those that come under the general heading of **extrasensory perception**, and those of a physical nature. The latter group includes *psychokinesis*, where physical objects are apparently able to move or change shape when willed to by an individual (eg spoon bending), and the so-called *poltergeist phenomenon*, where objects appear to be violently hurled about with no apparent cause. Psychologists are divided as to whether parapsychology can be considered a respectable branch of psychology. It deals with phenomena that seem to defy the known theories of science, and the experiments that have been designed to test the phenomena can rarely come up with the same results when repeated. It is probably fair to say that most psychologists – including many who are involved in parapsychology – are sceptics on the subject. However, no generally accepted explanations in line with orthodox science have been put forward.
See also **precognition; telepathy**

## passive-aggressive

A term used in two slightly different ways. In *passive-aggressive personality*, it describes a person who is very dependent, does not initiate action, but often responds to events in an aggressive way. In *passive-aggressive behaviour*, it refers to the type of behaviour patterns often shown by someone in a subservient position to those in superior positions, where **aggression** is expressed in actions that are not overtly hostile. For example, a cook who resents her employer may subtly oversalt all the food.

## Pavlovian

See **classical conditioning**

## peak experience

A term invented by the American psychologist Abraham Maslow (1908–70), and associated with **humanistic psychology**. It describes a moment when a person feels in deep harmony both with himself or herself and with the surrounding world. Although there is a sense of clarity of thought and perception, awareness of time and space are often diminished. The experience is closely related to Maslow's theory of **self-actualization**.

### penis envy

In **Freudian** theory, the hypothesis that all women have a repressed desire to have a penis. It is related to the female **castration complex**, the result of girl children discovering their anatomical difference from boys and imagining that they have somehow been deprived of a penis. According to Freud, women deal with this desire to possess a penis either through having children or by sexual intercourse with males. Only the most orthodox Freudians now accept this theory in its entirety; it is generally considered to be a product of Freud's so-called 'phallocentric' bias, which emphasizes the importance of the penis and sees women as being incomplete. The term penis envy is also sometimes used of the envy that young boys feel for the penis of grown men.

### performance tests

In various branches of **applied psychology**, tests that do not rely on verbal ability; also called **non-verbal tests**. Performance tests often involve picture completion, mazes, and various puzzles based on physical manipulation of objects. Scores on such tests tend to decline over the years.

### persona

A term in **Jungian** theory. It comes from the Latin word meaning 'person', but specifically refers to the stylized masks worn by actors in the classical Roman theatre that signified the roles they were playing. The persona, in Jung's terminology, is a person's public face, or the personality that people choose to project in their dealings with the world. The idea of the mask suggests that this public image may be a facade, disguising the true self or **anima**.

### personality

A term used very widely in many branches of psychology. Despite its central importance in psychology, it is one of those terms which defies precise definition, but most attempts at definition come close to the usual way in which lay people use the word, referring to the totality of qualities – motivational, emotional, behavioural – that distinguish an individual.

People have been forming theories of personality, and categorizing personality types, for centuries. One of the earliest theories was based on the idea of 'humours' or bodily fluids that influence whether a person is melancholic (see **melancholia**), choleric, sanguine, or phlegmatic. Even this theory, which dominated medieval thought, was sophisticated enough to take account of the fact that most people are a mixture of the various types and cannot be rigidly categorized. Probably the most influential of modern theories of personality types has been Jung's division into **extravert** and **introvert**. General theories of personality include the **psychoanalytical** approaches, particularly the **Freudian** theory of the **ego, id**, and **superego**; the trait theories of William McDougall (1871–1938) and R B Cattell (1905– ), which attempt to distinguish individual differences in personality traits; and social theories, which analyze personality within its social context. Modern theories of personality tend to be eclectic, drawing on many of the established theories.

## personality disorder

A very general diagnostic term that covers many kinds of psychological disorder. It has for many years been associated with disorders that cause antisocial or inadequate behaviour, rather than those that cause the sufferer deep psychological distress. The use of the term has, however, gradually narrowed down to mean a mental disorder in which the nature of an individual's patterns of thought and perception are liable to impair that person's social relationships and functioning and require treatment. Some of the disorders included are *paranoid personality disorders* (see **paranoia**), *schizoid personality disorders* (see **schizophrenia**), **narcissism, megalomania, antisocial personality**, and **obsessive-compulsive disorder**.

## personality test

Any device that is designed to measure or assess any aspect of human **personality**. Some tests are intended to give a general view of the subject's personality traits; others try to assess specific aspects, such as tolerance, creativity, or leadership abilities. Tests can be loosely divided into the direct question-and-answer variety, such as the **Minnesota Multiphasic Personality Inventory**, and indirect tests that use **projective techniques**.

## personal space

A term used in **social psychology** for the actual physical space that surrounds each individual, and which people regard as their own space which is not to be invaded against their will. People's attitude to their personal space varies according to situations and culture. Close friends and relations are not usually seen as hostile when they invade one's personal space, whereas a stranger might not come as close but will be seen as threatening. In an overcrowded country like India the amount of space most people feel that they can claim would be very much smaller than would be the case for people in a less populated country.
See also **territoriality**

## person perception

In **social psychology**, a term covering the ways in which people perceive other people. This includes people's assessment of other people's physical appearance, the way people form impressions of others, **attribution**, and the influence of prejudices in the way people are viewed.

## perversion

A word deriving from Latin *pervertere* 'turning the wrong way'; the sense is always somehow connected with diverting from the right course or misusing something. In psychological terminology, as in ordinary speech, the term has come to be identified with sexual perversion.

Traditionally, both in **psychoanalysis** and **psychiatry**, sexual perversion encompassed all deviation from the central act of intercourse between two people of different sexes, where the aim is genital penetration and orgasm. In **psychoanalytic theory**, sexual perversions were said to result from a failure to deal successfully with the various stages of psychosexual development, and were variously described as a **regression** to **infantile sexuality** or a **defence mechanism** against **anxiety**. In traditional psychiatry sexual perversions were considered to be forms of **personality disorder**. More recently it has been fairly generally accepted that human sexuality is extremely complex and that there are innumerable difficulties in trying to define 'normal' sexual acts or feelings. Hence, the term perversion is now largely used only for sexual acts that interfere with the rights of other adults or are directed towards children (eg rape, paedophilia, indecent exposure). **Homosexuality, sado-masochism, transvestism** and other areas once considered perversions are no longer thought to be such, provided that all those involved are consenting adults.

## petrification

A term in **Laingian** theory; literally 'turning into stone'. Laing uses the term to describe the way people who are insecure about their personal identity defend themselves against perceived threats to their identity. Either such people use petrification on themselves, depersonalizing themselves as a defensive device so that they feel safe from the threat posed by others; or they can choose to turn others to stone, depersonalizing them so they become things rather than people and are no longer threatening.

## phallic character

In **psychoanalysis**, a person who is **fixated** at the **phallic stage**, usually as the result of an unresolved **Oedipus complex**. The adult displays a phallic character in relation to sexual behaviour, regarding sex as a matter of potency and performance rather than in terms of personal relationships.

## phallic stage

In **psychoanalysis**, the stage of psychosexual development that follows the **anal stage** and precedes the **latency period** and the final **genital stage**. Children at this stage are preoccupied with interest in the genitals. For both sexes this means the penis, so that while boys are obsessed with their own penises (and liable to **castration complex**), girls are aware of their deficiency and develop **penis envy** (or, according to some theorists, use the clitoris as a penis substitute). It is also at this stage that the **Oedipus complex** appears and is, ideally, resolved.
See also **phallic character**

## phallic symbol

Anything that might be thought to represent the penis. The idea of the *phallus* as a symbolic representation of fertility and sexual power originated in anthropology, but was adopted by **psychoanalysts**, particularly with reference to such symbolism occurring in dreams and **fantasy**. It is part of the popular conception of psychoanalysis that everything more or less long and thin or upright – a cigarette, a snake, an express train, an obelisk – is interpreted as a phallic symbol. However, the concept is used very much more conservatively than is popularly believed, and even Freud is credited with saying that 'sometimes a cigar is really just a cigar'.

### phantasy
See **fantasy**

### phobia
An excessive and irrational fear of a particular object or situation; from Greek *phobos* 'fear'. Many people dislike spiders or would rather not be on an exposed mountain top or have an injection. However, they would not be classed as suffering from a phobia unless the fear was very intense and accompanied by **anxiety** symptoms such as the desire to flee or avoid the situation, sweating, palpitations, faintness, and so on. Also the fear must be irrational or out of proportion to any genuine threat or danger. It would be normal for anyone to experience acute anxiety symptoms if faced by a pack of Rottweilers, but only a sufferer from *cynophobia* (fear of dogs) would experience such symptoms when meeting a friend's miniature poodle. The most common phobias are **agoraphobia, acrophobia, claustrophobia, social phobia**, fear of animals, spiders, thunderstorms, and the dark, but there are many less common phobias, such as fear of beards (*pogonophobia*), feathers (*pteronophobia*), or rust (*iophobia*).

Phobias can often dominate sufferers' lives, limiting their opportunities and experiences: for example someone might turn down the offer of a good job because it would mean using a lift. The cause of phobia is often thought to be some unpleasant or distressing incident in the past that either actually involved the feared object or situation, or that has become unconsciously linked with it. Treatment is usually by some form of **behaviour modification**, often **desensitization**, or by **group therapy** or other forms of **psychotherapy**.

### phobic character
A term in **psychoanalysis**, used to describe a person who deals with all situations that are threatening or likely to produce

anxiety by avoiding them. Such people usually seek a protective home environment and rarely venture from it, restricting their activities to those that are guaranteed to be safe. There are also *counter-phobic characters* – people who deliberately seek out dangerous situations and activities that would cause anxiety in most people.

## physiological psychology

A branch of psychology that studies the physiological basis for behaviour; also called **biological psychology, psychobiology**, or **psychophysiology**. Emphasis is particularly on the nervous system and its operations in relation to such areas as learning, perception, and memory.

## Piagetian theory /ˈpjæʒeɪən/ *or* /pjæˈʒɛtiən/

Theories of **developmental psychology** associated with the Swiss psychologist Jean Piaget (1896–1980), who has been a major influence in **child psychology** and **educational psychology**. The most important of his theories is that concerned with the development of cognitive ability in children, who Piaget believed pass through successive stages of development: **sensorimotor, preoperational, concrete operations**, and **formal operations**. Piaget recognized that children think in a different way from adults, and that younger children think in a different way from older children. Children's responses and abilities have to be considered within the context of their developmental stage, and each stage must be allowed to take its course without adults attempting to interfere by accelerating the child's learning development. Piaget also did important research in the area of children's **moral development**.
See also **accommodation; assimilation; conservation; egocentrism; schema**

## pica

See **eating disorders**

## placebo effect /pləˈsiːbəʊ/

A *placebo* is a harmless preparation which would not be expected to have any physiological effect, but which is prescribed for its psychological effect in making a patient feel that something is being done for him or her, or which is used as a control in drug experiments; from Latin *placere* 'to please'. The term placebo effect was originally used in physiology to describe the phenomenon of a patient's symptoms apparently improving as a reaction to the use of a placebo. It has been extended in psychology to refer to any situation where people react positively to being given some form of attention or experimental treatment, where it is believed that the effect is caused by the attention given rather than by the specific treatment involved. See also **double blind; Hawthorne effect**

## play therapy

The use of play in **psychotherapy**, either for diagnosis or treatment. **Psychoanalysts** working with children use play as a substitute for **free association**, interpreting the child's emotional situation by the use it makes of toys. Play therapy as treatment usually involves allowing children to play freely so as to express inhibited emotions. Play therapy is normally used only with children, but some therapists use forms of play therapy with adults.

## pleasure principle

In **Freudian psychoanalysis**, the theory that mental functioning is governed by the desire to procure pleasure by gratifying the **drives** of the **id**, and to avoid pain or 'unpleasure' (the theory is also known as the **pleasure-pain** or **pleasure-unpleasure principle**). Before the **ego** has developed, the pleasure principle operates through **wish-fulfilment** or **fantasy** by which the child avoids the tension caused by being unable to satisfy its desires. The primitive pleasure principle eventually becomes modified by the **reality principle**.

## Pollyanna mechanism

A term for the **defence mechanism** used by people who exhibit unrealistic optimism and irrepressible cheerfulness, insisting that there is nothing wrong with them or with their situation when it is evident to others that there is. The name is taken from the heroine of Eleanor Porter's children's book *Pollyanna* (1913), who always looked on the bright side, and throughout various trials and tribulations persisted in finding 'something to be glad about'.

## positive reinforcement

In **conditioning**, the process of increasing the likelihood that a particular response or piece of behaviour will recur in the same circumstances by rewarding it. For example, a rat that turns left in a maze and is rewarded by finding some food will tend to turn left on subsequent occasions, having been positively reinforced for doing so.

## positive transfer

The phenomenon whereby skills and knowledge acquired in learning a particular task have the effect of improving performance when learning a different task. For example, having learned to ride a bicycle, it would be easier subsequently to learn to ride a motor cycle.

See also **negative transfer**

## post-hypnotic suggestion

See **hypnosis**

## post-traumatic stress disorder (PTSD)

A psychological disorder occurring in people who have experienced very stressful events such as natural disasters, travel accidents, or fires, or been victims of crime or terrorism. Typical symptoms are re-experiencing the situation in dreams, recurrent and distressing recollections and images, and flashback experiences; attempts to nullify the experience through loss of memory, feelings of estrangement and detachment, and numbing of emotions; and physical symptoms such as insomnia, irritability, and **anxiety** reactions in situations that recall the stressful experience. The usual treatment of PTSD is through **counselling, behaviour modification**, and **psychotherapy**.

See also **combat fatigue; gross stress reaction**

## precognition

A form of **extrasensory perception** in which someone has knowledge of a future event, without using the usual senses and without using logical inferences or deduction from existing knowledge in making the prediction. As precognition often occurs in dreams, visions, or **trance** states, it is difficult to test claims in an experimental situation.

## preconscious

In **psychoanalysis**, a term applied to thoughts, emotions, images, and so on that are not actually in a person's consciousness at a given time, but are easily accessible. Such thoughts and emotions are not repressed, and so are easy to recall when necessary.

## prefrontal lobotomy

See **lobotomy**

## preoperational stage

In **Piagetian theory**, the child's second **developmental stage**, usually starting at about 2 and ending at about 7 years of age. It begins with the establishment of *object permanence*, where the child realizes that objects are permanent and continue to exist regardless of whether the child is looking at them. At this stage children begin to organize their thoughts verbally, but thinking is still intuitive rather than logical, and the child still tends towards **egocentrism**.

## presenile dementia

See **Alzheimer's disease**

## primal scene

In **psychoanalysis**, sexual intercourse between parents as actually witnessed or, more often, as inferred by the child and incorporated into its **fantasies**. It is thought that the young child usually interprets the scene as an act of aggression by the father.

## primal therapy

A form of **psychotherapy**, also known as *primal scream therapy*, popular in the 1970s and based on the theories of the American psychologist Arthur Janov. The therapist guides patients in recalling and then reliving particularly painful and distressing experiences from childhood. They are then encouraged to recognize the emotions of anger and hurt, particularly in connection with their parents, that they have been repressing throughout their adult lives. The **breakthrough** to be aimed at is the expression of these emotions in a 'primal scream', a primitive and infantile yell of rage that is supposed to have a cathartic effect (see also **abreaction**).

## primary drive

A **drive** that arises from the physiological nature of a human being or animal; opposed to **acquired drives**, which are learned. The most basic primary drives are universal: to satisfy hunger and thirst, to avoid pain, to sleep. Other drives are less obviously universal but are included as primary drives, for example sex, curiosity, and maternal behaviour. Some primary drives – such as nest-building – are specific to particular species.

## primary gain

Generally, the benefit or gain derived by a patient in first developing some disorder. The term is used specifically in **psychoanalysis** to refer to the initial gain to the patient in developing a **neurosis**, in terms of lessening of **anxiety**.
See also **flight into illness; secondary gain**

## projection

A term whose literal meaning is connected with 'throwing forward'; all of its meanings in **psychiatry** and **psychoanalysis** are somehow connected with externalizing things that are internal. The standard meaning in psychoanalysis is the **defence mechanism** whereby one ascribes one's own feelings, wishes, and characteristics to someone else. In this way one relieves **anxiety** by denying these emotions or traits in oneself, but acknowledges their existence by projecting them on to another person. In **Kleinian** theory, projection does not involve **denial**, but is a normal developmental process: the infant projects its own feelings of anger on to the mother and then perceives her as hostile and rejecting. Another use of the term is more common in psychiatry, where projection usually refers to the way in which people interpret their surroundings, environment, other people and so on according to their own emotional state, personality, and disposition. It is this meaning that is relevant to the use of **projective techniques**.

## projective techniques

Procedures used for psychological testing and designed to ascertain information about a patient's **personality, motivation**, etc. The tests usually present patients with more or less unstructured material which they are free to interpret, their response supposedly giving insight into their personality and emotional state. Patients may be asked to interpret or describe a shape or a representative picture, or to complete a story or picture. Standardized tests using projective techniques include the Rorschach (see **inkblot test**) and the **Thematic Appperception Test**. **Play therapy** used as a diagnostic device can also be thought of as a projective method.

## psyche /'saɪki/

Greek, 'soul'. The term was first used to denote a life force, then to mean the mind or the self. Freud used it to mean the mind, and it is sometimes used as such in **psychoanalysis**, where *psychic* merely means 'mental' and has no connection with **parapsychology**. However, *psyche* is most often used as a prefix in the many words starting with *psych-* (see below).

## psychiatrist

Someone who practises **psychiatry** professionally. A psychiatrist is always a person who has qualified as a doctor, with a general medical training, and has then specialized in psychiatry. The psychiatrist's work may often overlap with that of the clinical **psychologist** or the **psychotherapist**, but unlike them (unless they are also qualified physicians) the psychiatrist can prescribe **drug therapy** for patients.

## psychiatry

The branch of medicine that deals in mental disorders and disturbances; from Greek *psyche* 'mind' + *iātros* 'physician'. Psychiatry includes research into and treatment of all illnesses whose symptoms are mental, even if the origins of the illness are physical (such as in **senile dementia**). It concentrates on abnormal behaviour and mental states, and the **psychiatrist** does not usually have psychological training covering normal mental development. While some psychiatrists accept **psychoanalysis** and other psychotherapeutic techniques, treatment within psychiatry is more likely to be physical, using **drug therapy** and sometimes **electroconvulsive therapy**.

## psychic

See **psyche**

## psychoanalysis

A theory of human behaviour and a form of **psychotherapy** invented by Sigmund Freud (see **Freudian**). Strictly speaking the term is limited to Freudian theory, but it can also be applied more loosely to subsequent theories and methods that have diverted somewhat from classic Freudian ideas but retain an emphasis on the **unconscious, free association, transference**, and interpretation by the therapist. As a form of therapy, psychoanalysis requires considerable commitment on the part of the patient, who is required to attend hourly sessions usually three or four times a week for around five years, and who must pay substantial fees. Psychoanalytic treatment within the National Health Service is very rarely an option in Britain.

## psychoanalyst

A practitioner of **psychoanalysis**. Psychoanalysts may have medical training and have trained in **psychiatry** or may have a background in psychology, **counselling**, or none of these. What is important is that they have had a full training at a recognized institute of psychoanalysis. This will normally involve the prospective psychoanalysts themselves undergoing Freudian psychoanalysis five days a week for five or six years before beginning analysis of patients under the supervision of more experienced practitioners (see **training analysis**). Those analysts who have had a rather less rigorous training or who are not orthodox Freudians, but employ the techniques of psycho-analysis, often refer to themselves as *analytic psychotherapists* rather than psychoanalysts.

## psychoanalytic theory

See **psychoanalysis**

## psychobiology

See **physiological psychology**

## psychodrama

A form of **psychotherapy** invented by the Austrian-born American psychiatrist J L Moreno (1890–1974). Patients are asked to act out a dramatic role which relates to their own particular conflicts and problems. Other roles are usually taken by the therapist or members of a therapeutic team. In *group psychodrama*, roles are played by other patients, and the subject of the drama is one that has emotional significance for all the patients in the group. Psychodrama is designed to help patients to express their emotions and gain insight into their problems. Therapists often ask players to exchange roles, so that a patient is enabled to react to his or her own situation objectively.

See also **role play**

## psycholinguistics

The study of the psychological aspects of language. These include the basic structure of language and its underlying grammar, the acquisition of language by children, the use of language, and the relationship between thought and language. Psycholinguistic issues also arise in the study of memory, learning, **information processing**, etc.

## psychologist

A theorist, researcher, or practitioner of psychology (in its wide definition as the study of mind and behaviour). Typically a professional psychologist will have studied for a first degree in psychology and have then proceeded to further training in academic psychology, **abnormal** or **clinical psychology**, or in one of the branches of **applied psychology**. It is unusual for a psychologist to have medical training.

## psychometrics

The area concerned with psychological measures or tests. This includes the design and standardization of such measures as **intelligence tests** and **personality tests**, the administering of such tests, and the analysis of the results. This last aspect often involves the use of sophisticated statistical techniques as much as psychological theories.

## psychopathic personality

The term *psychopath* literally means 'one suffering from a disorder of the mind', and was formerly applied to anyone with a severe mental disorder requiring treatment. It later became amended to *psychopathic personality*, and was applied specifically to what were once known as 'moral imbeciles': people who behave in an aggressive and antisocial manner, having no sense of moral and social obligations or the rights of others, and apparently experiencing no anxiety or guilt in relation to their behaviour. The term is now losing popularity in diagnosis, and many people who would have come into this category are now labelled as suffering from an **antisocial personality** disorder.

**psychopathology**
See **abnormal psychology**

**psychophysiology**
See **physiological psychology**

**psychosis**
Severe mental disturbance, from Greek *psyche* 'mind' + *osis* 'abnormal condition'. The term applies to serious mental illnesses that are of physical origin (eg resulting from brain damage) as well as those of emotional origin. Psychiatrists and psychoanalysts no longer use the words 'mad' or 'insane', but at one time would roughly divide mentally ill patients into the psychotic – who were clearly mad – and the neurotic, who were disturbed or distressed but sane. In fact, the word psychosis is itself now rarely used, having been replaced by *psychotic disorder*. The most significant characteristic of the psychotic disorders is a loss of reality. Patients persist in misinterpreting both external reality and their own thoughts and perceptions, typically refusing to acknowledge that they are ill. **Delusions, hallucinations**, and **inappropriate affect** are all typical symptoms. The major psychotic disorders are **manic depression, paranoia**, and **schizophrenia**.

**psychosomatic disorders**
A term covering all disorders where physical symptoms are assumed to arise from emotional causes; from Greek *psyche* 'mind' + *soma* 'body'. Some of the physical illnesses most often cited as being due to **stress** and other emotional factors are migraine, asthma, and stomach ulcers. However, the term *psychosomatic* is falling into disfavour. Labelling an illness a psychosomatic disorder often leads patients and their families to think that this means that the illness is somehow not genuine, and that there is some element of malingering, whereas this is of

course not the case. Also, the medical profession is increasingly coming to believe that virtually all illnesses are affected more or less by the patient's psychological state, and so it is inappropriate to label particular disorders as psychosomatic.

## psychosurgery
See **lobotomy**

## psychosynthesis
A form of **psychotherapy** invented by the Italian psychoanalyst Roberto Assagioli (1888–1974). It uses psychoanalytic techniques, more along **Jungian** than **Freudian** lines, to foster the development of a well-integrated personality and to help people realize their higher nature and purpose in life. Assagioli believed that people repress their sublime instincts as much as their base ones, and should be encouraged to recognize them. Psychosynthesis is characterized by an emphasis on health rather than pathology, and by an absence of rigid orthodoxy – it is a continually developing approach.

## psychotherapist
A person who practises **psychotherapy**. As psychotherapy covers such a huge field, the fact that someone is a psychotherapist tells one very little about what background and training he or she has had, and what kind of treatment he or she is offering. Some psychotherapists are trained in **psychiatry** or **clinical psychology**, some have a background in **counselling** or social work, and some have trained at an institute specializing in their particular form of therapy. However, in most countries there is no legal requirement for those calling themselves psychotherapists to have any particular training at all.

## psychotherapy
A very broad term, covering all forms of treatment of emotional and psychological disturbance and disorder by psychological, rather than physical, methods. Psychotherapy can be carried out individually or in a group, and can be long-term or short-term, but it is usually based on talking and on the therapist-patient relationship. **Psychoanalysts** are divided as to whether psychoanalysis is a form of psychotherapy. Some maintain that it is, while others make a sharp distinction between psycho-

analysis and psychotherapy. However, it is certainly the case that many forms of psychotherapy employ the theories and techniques of psychoanalysis, if sometimes in modified form. Other forms of psychotherapy are based on **behaviour modification** techniques; yet others are based on **humanistic psychology**. As psychotherapy covers so many forms of treatment, from the well-established and orthodox to the bizarre, it is wise to find out exactly what is on offer when psychotherapy is suggested.

## psychotic disorder
See **psychosis**

## pyromania
An uncontrollable instinct to start fires; from Greek *pȳr* 'fire' + **mania**. It is classed as an **impulse-control disorder**, and is characterized by a fascination with lighting fires and watching them burn. The pyromaniac lights fires solely with the motive of fulfilling the urge to do so, rather than with any motive such as revenge or in order to make a fraudulent insurance claim.

# R

### racial unconscious
See **collective unconscious**

### rapid eye movements
See **REM-sleep**

### rapport
A term used in a very similar way to how it is used in everyday English, for a friendly comfortable relationship between people. Within the context of **psychoanalysis, psychotherapy,** and **counselling**, it is usually applied to the relationship that ideally develops between the analyst, therapist, or counsellor and the client or patient – involving **empathy** on the one hand, and trust on the other.

### rational emotive therapy
A form of **cognitive behaviour modification**, invented by the American psychologist Albert Ellis (1913– ). It is an extremely directive form of therapy, based on the idea that emotional problems are rooted in irrational belief systems. The therapist confronts patients with the irrationality of their ideas, and forcefully attempts to persuade them to think and behave in a more rational and realistic manner.

### rationalization
In **psychoanalysis**, a **defence mechanism** whereby people attempt to justify themselves and hide their true motivations by providing rational and logical explanations and interpretations for their feelings and behaviour. For example, a father who is jealous of his wife's affection for their son might rationalize his harsh behaviour to the boy by telling himself that young men need to learn discipline and independence.

### reactance theory
A theory in **social psychology** which claims that people will react to a restriction or an attempt to control their choices and

decisions by desiring to do whatever it is that is prohibited or to choose the very thing that they are being directed away from. An example is the phenomenon sometimes known as the *Romeo and Juliet effect*, in which young people's mutual attraction is strengthened by parental opposition to their relationship.

### reaction-formation
In **psychoanalysis**, a **defence mechanism** in which people cope with unacceptable impulses and desires by repressing them and then exhibiting **attitudes** and behaviour directly opposed to them. For example, an unfailingly kind and respectful demeanour towards one's father may be a reaction-formation against one's hatred of him; an exaggerated distaste for the company of young children may be a reaction-formation against paedophile tendencies.

### reactive depression
See **depression**

### reading disability
A general term in **educational psychology** for a failure to learn to read that is significant enough to place a child two or more years behind his or her peer group in ability. Also known as **reading disorder** or **reading difficulty**. It is a less specific term than **dyslexia**, and although dyslexic children would be included, the category also covers children whose reading problem is associated with general low intellectual ability, language problems, emotional problems, or a poor home environment, although not those who are mentally retarded or suffer from severe physical handicap.

### reality orientation
A form of therapy widely used in residential homes for old people, and aimed at treating the confusion, disorientation, and memory loss that result either from **senile dementia** or just from the normal process of aging. Reality orientation uses various pieces of equipment and games in structured learning sessions. These are designed to stimulate, for example, the old people's senses and memory, their sense of time and the appropriate timetables for daily living, and their recognition of ordinary household items and how they are used.

## reality principle

In **Freudian** theory, one of the two principles that govern all mental functioning, the other being the **pleasure principle**. The reality principle works as a brake and regulator to the pleasure principle. As a child's **ego** develops, he or she gradually learns to modify and adapt the basic desires of the **id** so that they correspond more to the facts of the external world, and have a better chance of being fulfilled in reality rather than by **wish fulfilment**.

## recall

A term used in two ways by psychologists studying the area of memory. It describes the process of information retrieval whereby one can call to mind a previous experience, such as repeating the words of a poem once learned or bringing to mind an image of a friend's house. It also describes the experimental situation in which the subjects are given something to learn, and the experimenter tests their ability to reproduce the material.

## reference group

In **social psychology**, a group with which a person feels a sense of identification, and which acts as a source or guide for his or her beliefs, values, **attitudes**, and behaviour. The group may be a small one (such as a family or a clique at school) or a large one (such as a social class or ethnic group). The person in question may not actually be a member of the group or be accepted by it, in which case he or she is likely to conform even more closely to the group's norms in the hope of being accepted. In speaking of such situations, psychologists sometimes use the term *aspirational reference group*.

## regression

A word with several meanings in psychology, all associated with the meaning of 'going backwards'. The most important use of the term, and the one most likely to be encountered, is as a description of a person reverting to an earlier form of behaviour or thought patterns. An adult who has started to act like an adolescent, or a 10-year-old child who is suddenly behaving like an infant, are said to be *regressing*. In **psychoanalysis**, regression is regarded as a **defence mechanism**: in order to avoid **anxiety** and conflict, a person regresses to an earlier stage of psychosexual or **ego** development. In **psychiatry** and psycho-analysis, regression is always regarded as a symptom of distur-bance or a neurotic reaction, but in some contexts it has a less negative status. Some **psychotherapists** encourage patients to regress during therapeutic sessions, in order to relive childhood experiences and emotions. Some theories of **cognitive devel-opment** see regression to earlier thought patterns as a some-times necessary stage in the progression to more advanced cognitive functioning.

## reinforcement

A term used in various ways, but all referring to the strengthen-ing or supporting of a piece of behaviour, usually within the context of learning. In **conditioning**, reinforcement refers to the unconditioned stimulus when presented at more or less the same time as the conditioned stimulus. Reinforcement is often used synonymously with **positive reinforcement**, and also with 'reward'.

## relaxation therapy

**Psychotherapy** that uses physical relaxation techniques in order to relieve emotional **stress** and tension. The patient is usually trained in relaxing groups of muscles, one at a time. Relaxation therapy is often used as part of **behaviour modifi-cation** approaches such as **desensitization**.

## release therapy

Any form of **psychotherapy** that encourages patients to release bottled-up emotions by an open expression of anger, hostility, or grief, in the belief that this will help them to cope with their feelings or reach a level of self-understanding. Therapies that make use of this approach include **Gestalt therapy, primal therapy**, and **psychodrama**.

## REM-sleep

('Rapid eye movement sleep'.) The period of sleep when the sleeper's eyes can be observed to be moving in a quick and jerky manner, and characteristic changes in heart-beat and respiration can be measured. The most significant fact about REM-sleep is that it seems almost always to be accompanied by dreaming. Most people have three or four periods of REM-sleep, totalling about

90–120 minutes during an 8-hour period of sleep. Research into REM-sleep indicates that dreaming is an important human function, perhaps even a necessity. People repeatedly woken from REM-sleep will show more signs of disturbance than when woken from non-REM sleep, and will compensate by dreaming more when allowed to sleep uninterrupted.

## reparation

In **psychoanalysis**, the **defence mechanism** whereby people reduce guilt about their destructive thoughts and fantasies by doing good to the person against whom these hostile thoughts were directed. This is an important idea in **Kleinian** theory, where reparation is regarded as the usual way for people to cope with their ambivalent feelings.

## repetition compulsion

A term used in two quite different ways. Its usual meaning in **psychiatry** is an **obsessive-compulsive disorder** in which the patient feels compelled to go through the same piece of behaviour over and over again (eg compulsive checking or hand washing). In **psychoanalysis**, it refers to the patient's desire to revert to former emotional states, particularly as a sign of **resistance** against the insights gained through the therapeutic process.

## repression

An important term in **psychoanalysis**, but also used generally to mean the process whereby people protect themselves from **anxiety** and guilt by refusing to allow certain unacceptable or distressing memories, ideas, or images to become **conscious**. Not only do the memories and ideas remain **unconscious**, but the process by which they are relegated also operates at an unconscious level. In **Freudian** theory, repression is a **defence mechanism** and part of the **ego**'s function in controlling impulses from the **id**. Freud distinguishes between *primary repression*, which is the initial process of confining disturbing elements to the realm of the unconscious, and *secondary repression*, in which anything which might act as a reminder of these things is itself repressed. Repressed impulses and images appear in dreams and, according to Freud, are the basis for various neuroses.

## reproductive facilitation
See **facilitation**

## resistance
In **psychoanalysis**, the patient's opposition to the analyst bringing repressed material into consciousness. Patients may also resist the analyst's attempts to probe areas of **unconscious** conflict and to interpret material. Resistance sometimes takes the form of a **conscious** and overt refusal to supply information to the analyst, but it is usually unconscious and expressed in more subtle forms. Some degree of resistance is thought to be universal in all patients undergoing psychoanalysis. The term resistance is also sometimes used in the psychology of **personality** to describe the personality trait characterized by a reluctance to conform to group norms and to obey orders.

## resolution
A term used in various contexts to mean the solution of a problem. In areas of psychology concerned with problem-solving techniques and decision making, it refers to the bringing together of the various elements of a problem to achieve a workable solution. In **psychotherapy** and **counselling**, it refers to the patient or client coming to a position where he or she feels able to understand and cope with a particular problem or conflict.

## role
In **social psychology**, the behaviour patterns which an individual is expected to perform in particular social situations; from French *rôle*, literally the roll of paper on which an actor's part in a play was written. People's roles change throughout their lives, and most people are playing several roles at once. Within the course of a day, for example, someone might be called upon to play the roles of mother, wife, boss, employee, and patient, and be expected to behave differently in each role.

## role conflict
The conflict in which a person has to play two or more **roles** which are incompatible. For example, a schoolteacher whose own child is in his class may have a conflict between his roles as firm, assertive teacher and loving, easy-going father.

## role play

A term sometimes used to mean the playing out of one's appropriate and expected **role**, or the deliberate playing of a different role. However, its usual meaning is the guided acting out of a particular role, in order to come to a better understanding of the thoughts, lives, motives, and emotions of oneself and others. Such role play is used in many therapeutic situations, particularly in **psychodrama** and various forms of **group therapy**. It is also used in educational settings and in various forms of industrial and professional training.

## Rorschach test

See **inkblot test**

## Rosenthal effect

In **social** and **experimental psychology**, a phenomenon that illustrates both **experimenter bias** and **self-fulfilling prophecy**. The American psychologist Robert Rosenthal (1933– ) conducted an experiment in which he told teachers that certain children in their classes had particularly high **IQ**s, although in fact the children were of average ability. In the following year these children were found to have performed better than average, presumably as a result of the teachers' attitude towards them and expectations.

# S

## sadism

Obtaining sexual pleasure and gratification from inflicting physical pain or humiliation on another person. The word derives from the name of the French writer, the Marquis de Sade (1740–1814), who both indulged in and wrote about such practices. It is sometimes used outside the sexual context to mean simply enjoyment of cruelty and the exercise of power. In some **psychoanalytic** theories, particularly **Kleinian**, it is used more or less synonymously with **aggression**.
See also **masochism; sado-masochism**

## sado-masochism

The combination of **sadism** and **masochism**. Although they appear to be polar opposites, these tendencies are often found in the same person. Many theorists believe that they are closely related, and that masochism is a manifestation of sadistic impulses, turned upon oneself. The adjective *sado-masochistic* is also used to describe **fantasies** containing both sadistic and masochistic elements, and to describe a relationship where the partners adopt the role of sadist and masochist; sometimes the roles are permanent, sometimes the relationship involves the partners reversing roles.

## satyriasis /sætɪˈraɪəsɪs/

Excessive, obsessive, and exaggerated sexual desire in men; from the *satyrs* of Greek mythology: minor goatlike wood-gods who accompanied Dionysus (or Bacchus), the god of wine and revelry, and were noted for their wild and lascivious behaviour. Like women with **nymphomania**, men with satyriasis are not simply people who enjoy sex, or even people who are extremely promiscuous. The condition is also sometimes called *Don Juanism* (after the legendary Spanish philanderer), a reference to the desire to seduce one woman after another, never forming affectionate relationships, and never achieving satisfaction.

## scapegoat

An innocent person or  group unjustly blamed for the faults of others. The word is a translation of a Hebrew word, meaning 'goat of Azazel', and refers to the ancient custom of choosing a goat, dedicating it to the demon Azazel, and symbolically burdening it with all the sins of the Jewish people before releasing it into the wilderness (Leviticus 16.5–10). In individuals, using a scapegoat is a form of **defence mechanism**, in which one's own frustrations, aggression, and inadequacies can be denied by blaming another person for all that goes wrong. A scapegoat can also be used by political leaders who want to divert the public from their own failures by blaming some specific group (eg Jews or immigrants) for all economic and other crises.

## schema /ˈskiːmə/

A term used in various contexts to refer to a mental plan or framework used for dealing with experiences and information, from Greek 'form'. It is often used within the context of **cognitive development**, and particularly in **Piagetian theory**, to describe the systems used by children at different stages to organize and interpret their thoughts and experiences.

## schizophrenia

A term used in **psychiatry** for various **psychotic** disorders; from Greek *schizo* 'split' + *phrenia* 'mind', an etymology that has probably been responsible for the confusion between this type of disorder and the much rarer one of split personality (see **multiple personality**). The splitting in schizophrenia is a disintegration of the functions of personality, a dissociation between the patient's thoughts and emotions. The onset of the illness is typically in young adulthood – or at least, before middle age – and common symptoms include **delusions, hallucinations, inappropriate affect**, illogical thinking, and a loss of contact with reality. The patient usually appears detached and unable to function socially or to relate to others.

Schizophrenia is often separated into different categories, according to what symptoms predominate. The main categories are: *hebephrenic* or *disorganized schizophrenia* (see **hebephrenia**), in which the main symptoms are childish and bizarre behaviour, delusions, and hallucinations; *catatonic schizophrenia* (see **catatonia**), where the patient is completely motionless for long periods of time, but will suddenly launch into frenzied activity;

*paranoid schizophrenia*, in which the main symptoms are delusions of persecution and jealousy; and *simple schizophrenia*, which is characterized by detachment and loss of normal emotional reactions. The terms *schizoid personality disorder* and *schizotypal personality disorder* refer to illnesses that share some of the characteristics of schizophrenia. The former involves emotional detachment and **withdrawal**, and the latter erratic thought and behaviour, but neither is thought of as a form of schizophrenia.

## screen memory

In **psychoanalysis**, a childhood memory that is both very clear and striking but apparently trivial in its content. The recollection may be false or distorted, but such memories are regarded as important because they are thought to symbolize significant elements of a person's childhood experiences and to be a cover for repressed childhood **fantasies** or events that they help to conceal.

## secondary drive

See **acquired drive**

## secondary gain

The continuing gain or advantage to the patient of having an illness, or specifically, a **neurosis**. It differs from **primary gain** in that it applies not to the relief from **anxiety** that accompanies the formative stages of the illness, but to the way in which a patient uses an established illness in order to manipulate others and avoid unpleasant duties and responsibilities.

## section

A term used in Great Britain to refer to various sections of the Mental Health Act, under which mentally ill people can be compulsorily detained in a mental hospital for a limited period of time. The word is actually used as a verb, to describe having someone committed to hospital, as in 'he was violent so we got the doctor in and he was sectioned'.

## self-actualization

A concept associated with the American psychologist Abraham Maslow (1908–70), but actually invented by Kurt Goldstein

(1878–1965), a German-born American theorist who used the term to mean the motive – for him, the primary human motive – to fulfil one's potential. For Maslow, self-actualization was not a motive but a level of development to be aimed at, incorporating independence and autonomy, tranquillity and confidence in dealing with one's environment and experiences, and the ability to form deep and lasting relationships. It is the desired goal of all forms of **psychotherapy** based on **humanistic psychology**. See also **peak experience**

## self-concept
A term used in various branches of psychology to mean the overall view and perception that people have of themselves. This encompasses everything that people think about themselves, and includes **self-esteem** and **self-image**.

## self-esteem
The value that people put on themselves. The term really means how much people like and respect themselves and expect others to like and respect them. Many psychological disorders, such as **depression**, are characterized by an unrealistically low self-esteem, where patients feel worthless and are unable to see any good or value in themselves. More unusually, in a disorder like **narcissism**, the patient's self-esteem is extremely high.

## self-fulfilling prophecy
A prediction of future events that is fulfilled – or turns out to happen – because of people holding prior convictions about the outcome and behaving in a way that is coloured by these beliefs. It is an important element in **experimenter bias**, where the result of an experiment is likely to be affected by the experimenter's expectations. Self-fulfilling prophecy is also found in less formal situations. For example, a child who is habitually treated as a potential criminal will very likely grow up to break the law, whereas one who is believed to be gifted, and encouraged by parents and teachers, will probably achieve well. See also **Rosenthal effect**

## self-image
The self that a person imagines him/herself to be, which is often

very much at variance with the objective perceptions that others would have about the person. One's self-image is usually formed at an early stage in one's life, and is closely related to one's **body image**. This early idea of oneself often persists into later life, although it may no longer be appropriate. So a slim, successful, and assertive woman may have retained the self-image that she formed when she was a shy and podgy little girl; a fat and balding middle-aged man may still see himself as the attractive young man he was 20 years ago.

## semantic satiation

*Semantic* means 'to do with meaning in language', while *satiation* is 'having enough, or more than enough, of something'. Semantic satiation is the term psychologists have given to a very common phenomenon that most people have experienced. If one takes any ordinary familiar word (try *kettle* or *what*) and repeats it over and over again, it will gradually come to seem totally meaningless. Having identified and named the phenomenon, psychologists have still not been able to come up with a sound explanation of it.

## senile dementia

**Dementia** occurring in old people. It is caused by atrophy of the brain with age, and is characterized by a progressive deterioration in memory, reasoning, and judgement, usually leading to death within 10 years. It is sometimes associated with the later stages of illnesses such as **Alzheimer's disease** or *Pick's disease*, but is sometimes just due to the natural aging processes.

## sensitive period

A term used in the psychology of learning, and applying both to human beings and animals. It refers to a period in an organism's development when that person or animal is optimally ready to respond to certain stimuli and/or to acquire certain skills, knowledge, or abilities. In human beings sensitive periods are as much influenced by psychological as physiological factors, and their duration is less well-defined than in animals. For example, the sensitive period for acquiring language lasts several years. In animals the phenomenon is biologically based, and the sensitive period can be a matter of hours, as in the best-known example – that of *imprinting*, where newly hatched ducks will follow the first object they are exposed to. Sensitive periods are also known as *critical periods*, particularly when applied to the sharply defined and physiologically determined animal examples, where if the response is not acquired during the critical period then it never will be.

## sensitivity training

A technique in which individuals gather for group discussion, with the aim of gaining a better understanding of **group dynamics** and interpersonal relationships, and becoming more sensitive to the feelings and motivations of themselves and others. The group is usually small and unstructured, though with a trained leader, and discussion is free and uninhibited. Groups that use sensitivity training include so-called *t-groups* ('t' stands for training) and *encounter groups*, where participants are encouraged to break down emotional barriers and develop trust in their relationships. Sensitivity training has its roots in the **human potential movement** and its techniques are based on those of **group therapy**. It is not, however, generally used as a therapeutic technique for the psychologically disordered, but more as a training in interpersonal skills for individuals in business and other organizations.

## sensorimotor stage

In **Piagetian theory**, the first **developmental stage** of a child's life, from birth until about 18 months or 2 years. During this stage children are primarily developing their sense perceptions and physical coordination. They start life by being entirely **egocentric**, but during this stage begin to develop the sense of other people being separate from themselves. The final achievement at this stage is the understanding of *object permanence* – the fact that objects continue to exist regardless of whether the child can see or touch them.

## separation anxiety

In **psychoanalysis**, the infant's anxiety about being separated from its mother or mother substitute. By extension it refers to later fears about separation from the security of home and parents or other carers. The anxiety does not need to relate to an actual situation of separation from the mother, but some theorists believe that actual experiences of **maternal deprivation** in early childhood can lead to psychiatric disorders. *Separation-anxiety disorder* is a disorder of children who are excessively fearful about leaving home and parents, worry about what might happen to their parents when they are away from them, and often develop *school phobia*.

## sex therapy

Any form of therapy that is designed to help people with sexual problems. It focuses mainly on problems of attitude towards sex – such as fear, guilt, or disgust – and **psychosomatic** physical problems such as impotence, vaginismus, or premature ejaculation.

## short-term memory

Memory for information that has only just been presented to one. Information is held in the short-term memory for only a matter of 15–30 seconds, after which it is forgotten or transferred to the **long-term memory**. It is thought that most people can hold only about seven items of information in their short-term memory at one time.

## sibling rivalry

The very common situation of competition and rivalry between siblings (ie brothers and sisters). The competition is usually for the affection and attention of parents. Typically, first-born children feel rivalry with a younger sibling who they fear will displace them in their parents' affections, while younger children are jealous of the perceived privileges and superior abilities of their older siblings.

## significant other

Originally, in psychology, a person who is particularly important and influential in forming someone's values, **attitudes**, and **self-image**. Generally the person is in a position of power, such as a parent, teacher, or group leader. The term is often used in a much vaguer sense, just to mean anyone who is important to someone, and has recently come to be used in the USA as a 'politically correct' synonym for girlfriend, boyfriend, or live-in lover, when it is sometimes abbreviated to **SO**.

## single-blind

In **experimental psychology**, the situation in which the subjects are kept ignorant of the details and purpose of the experiment, but the person conducting it does know. This is less effective in eliminating bias than the **double-blind**, but at least any biasing effect from the subjects' expectations is reduced.

## Skinnerian

Related to the theories of the American psychologist B F Skinner (1904–91). Skinner was the most famous advocate of **behaviourism**, and originated the theories of **operant conditioning**, which he applied to both animal and human learning. He invented the *Skinner Box* – a box to house experimental animals, fitted with levers or bars for the animal to press, a device from which food can be released, and often a floor through which electric shocks can be given. He also invented an early form of teaching machine, based on a theory of *programmed learning* in which students' learning is reinforced by immediate feedback when they give the correct response. Skinner extended his theories to every aspect of life, and wrote a novel, *Walden Two* (1948), describing a Utopian community founded on principles of social engineering.
See also **functional**

## sleep deprivation

A term applicable to any situation where people are deprived of sleep, for example, through chronic insomnia, unusual situations like excessive background noise, or as a torture or punishment imposed on prisoners. However, in psychology it is most likely to apply to an experimental situation in which volunteers are systematically deprived of normal sleep and their reactions are monitored. Effects of sleep deprivation include fatigue, as one might expect, and also loss of concentration, reduced performance at manual and intellectual tasks, irritability and other signs of **stress**, and sometimes **hallucinations**. Most of these effects are exacerbated if the subject is constantly woken during **REM-sleep**.

## sleeper effect

In **social psychology**, a change in attitude that occurs some time after a person has been exposed to information or propa-

---

ganda. Thus people may think that they have been totally unaffected by the message of an advertisement or a political broadcast, but the effect of their exposure to it may emerge some time later in their buying or voting behaviour.

**social exchange theory**
See **exchange theory**

**social facilitation**
The enhancement of performance, or stimulation of certain behaviour, caused by the presence of others. It is generally the case that people work harder, play more enthusiastically, and perform better when they have an audience or when there are other people engaging in similar activities nearby. This phenomenon is also seen in animals, who will, for example, eat even when not hungry if other animals of the same species are feeding.

**socialization**
The process by which people gradually learn to adapt to and fit in with the society in which they live. The term is used in many ways. Within **psychoanalytic** theory, socialization is a matter of a child internalizing the values of its parents and developing a **superego**. In other approaches, it is thought to be more a matter of children picking up the language, customs, and values of the society, often **modelling** themselves on others who have already acquired the necessary social skills and knowledge. Although the term is often applied to children, socialization is usually regarded as a lifelong process, and can be applied to specific situations encountered in life, for example, when someone moves to a different country or starts to work for a different organization, where new social norms have to be learned.

**social-learning theory**
A theory of how social behaviour and **personality** are developed, based mainly on the work of the American psychologist Albert Bandura (1925– ). According to this theory, children learn their social behaviour and develop their personality and moral principles primarily through observing others and **modelling** their behaviour and values on those of others.

## social phobia

Any of a number of **phobias** in which fear and anxiety is associated with general or specific social situations. Most people have known the experience of feeling shy or anxious about public-speaking or facing a room full of strangers, but sufferers from social phobia are quite incapacitated by their fear. Many are unable to work, cannot eat in a public place, and refuse all invitations to events where they will have to mix with other people. Treatment is usually in groups, and uses **behaviour modification** techniques and sometimes **assertiveness training**.

## social psychology

The branch of psychology that studies people in their social and cultural environments. It examines the ways in which people's **attitudes**, behaviour, and **personality** are influenced by the dynamics of the social groups which they belong to, aspire to, and interact with; the ways in which people relate to other people, groups and social institutions; and the ways in which people function within particular groups such as families, political or religious organizations, committees or work groups. There is often an overlap with sociology, but the emphasis in social psychology is on people and their behaviour within societies, rather than the actual structures of the societies themselves.

## sociometric test

A test using *sociometry*, a technique for measuring aspects of interpersonal relations that was invented by the American psychiatrist J L Moreno (1890–1974). A sociometric test typically measures what different members of a group think of each other. For example, schoolchildren might be asked to rate each of the other children in their class as to whether they like or dislike that person, would be happy to play with them or cooperate with them on a project, and so on. The researchers might analyse the result of such a test by constructing a *sociogram*, a diagram illustrating the relationships of likes and dislikes within the group. Sociometric tests are sometimes used to identify leaders or form a compatible working group; sometimes they are used in order to study what factors (eg intelligence, physical appearance, racial group) make for popularity or unpopularity.

## sour grapes mechanism

A **defence mechanism** whereby people convince themselves that a goal or object that they cannot achieve or obtain was really not worth having. It comes from the famous fable by Aesop in which a fox who was unable to reach some grapes declared that they were sour, and wouldn't have made good eating anyway.

## split personality

See **multiple personality**

## splitting

A term used in several different ways in **psychoanalysis**. Freud speaks of *splitting of the ego*, by which he means a **defence mechanism** in which a person dissociates one part of him/herself from the rest, regarding just the one part as the self and regarding the other part or parts as external. This can apply to the few genuine cases of **multiple personality**, but Freud also applied it to splits in the ego in various **psychoses** and in **fetishism**. The term *splitting of the object* is a feature of **Kleinian** psychoanalytical theory; in this case the splitting applies not to the self but to another person who is the object of ambivalent feelings, and is thus split into a 'good' and a 'bad' person.

## S-R

See **stimulus-response**

## stage theories

See **developmental stages**

## Stanford-Binet Scale

The popular adaptation of the original **Binet Scale**, which has become the most common English-language **intelligence test** used for testing **IQ**. It is called the Stanford-Binet as it was formulated at Stanford University in California in 1916. The test is largely used for children, but the various modernizations and revisions of it include scales for measuring adult IQ.

## stereotype

A metaphor taken from the printing industry, where a stereotype is a solid metal printing plate cast from a mould. In **social psychology** the word is used to mean a widely held but over-simplified, generalized, and uncritical idea about any group of people. Stereotypes are often applied to members of a particular race, class, occupational group, or gender. Typical stereotypes are the ideas that Germans are hard-working, fair-haired people with no sense of humour; women are emotional and poor at abstract reasoning; teachers are left-wing bossy people with pens in the top pockets of their tweed jackets. The word is also used as a verb: to stereotype people is to categorize them according to a preconceived idea about the group that they belong to.

## stimulus-response (S-R)

The relationship between something that affects an organism's behaviour (the *stimulus*) and the reaction (or *response*) that is associated with it. The term is frequently used as an adjective, linked to such nouns as *psychology, theory, learning*, to indicate that the approach being discussed is one that derives its principles from ideas of **conditioning** and **behaviourism**.

## Stockholm syndrome

The phenomenon whereby the victims of hostage-taking come to identify with their captors and develop positive and sometimes affectionate feelings towards them. The hostages come to see their all-powerful captors as kind if they refrain from ill-treating them, and not to blame if they are violent towards them. They become very negative towards the authorities who refuse the captors' demands and fail to rescue the hostages, blaming them for any violence that they suffer. The term originated with a bank robbery in Stockholm, where hostages were taken and a woman hostage developed a sexual relationship with one of her captors and subsequently became engaged to him. The phenomenon is also sometimes known as *hostage transference*.

## stress

A very general term in psychology used to apply to any strain or pressure, either psychological or physical, that disturbs the functioning of a person or animal. The term is used both for the cause – the strain put upon the organism – and the effect that the strain has, although the word *stressor* is sometimes used for the cause. Physical stress such as extremes of heat or cold, excessive noise or discomfort, result primarily in physical symptoms. Psychological and social stress such as frustrating situations, work pressure, or family conflicts are likely to produce both psychological tension – manifesting itself as **anxiety**, irritability, or **depression** – and physical symptoms.

## stress management

A term used in **psychotherapy** and **counselling** for techniques aimed at reducing the causes, and coping with the effects, of **stress**. Stress management is usually aimed at dealing with a particular situation that is causing the client or patient to experience tension, and tackling it by any of a variety of psychotherapeutic techniques, as well as physical therapies such as **relaxation therapy**.

## structuralism

A word used in many different ways, but in psychology *not* usually applied to the cultural anthropology movement that has been so influential in other fields, such as sociology and literary criticism. Its main use in psychology is to refer to the movement associated particularly with the German psychologist Wilhelm Wundt (1832–1920), which viewed the mind as a mental structure whose contents could be examined by means of introspection. It is often contrasted with the parallel movement of **functionalism** that emphasized the functions, rather than the contents, of the mind.

## subconscious

A term used generally in psychology to apply to memories and thoughts that are just below the level of consciousness, and could easily be brought into consciousness. In **psychoanalysis** it roughly corresponds to the term **preconscious**. Although the term is often particularly associated with psychoanalysis, it is not in fact actually used by most analysts, mainly because it has become so confused popularly with the idea of the **unconscious**.

## sublimation

The redirection of **unconscious** and unacceptable impulses into behaviour that is socially acceptable; from Latin *sublimis* 'elevated, exalted'. Although the term is used generally in psychology, its origin is in **psychoanalysis**, where it is classed as a **defence mechanism**, whereby the primitive aggressive and sexual energy of the **libido** becomes displaced and transformed into acceptable activities with no apparent sexual or aggressive elements involved. For Freud the classic example of activities that were the result of sublimation were intellectual curiosity and artistic creativity.

## superego

In **Freudian** theory, the third agency that (with the **ego** and **id**) makes up the human personality, and the last to develop. Partly **conscious** and partly **unconscious**, the superego acts as a sort of conscience or judge, punishing unacceptable thoughts or behaviour by feelings of guilt. Its development is the result of a child **internalizing** its parents' authority, prohibitions, and moral standards and also absorbing the ethical values of society. However, the superego is very often far more rigid, intolerant, and severe than are the parental or societal models from which it was derived, and can be irrational and impervious to changes in circumstances or society's standards.

## surrogate

In standard use, a substitute, or someone who takes the place of another. In psychology it is used similarly, but the emphasis is on psychological substitution. It is most frequently used to describe the situation where somebody becomes a mother surrogate or father surrogate for a child, or sometimes for an adult, taking on the role of a parent when for some reason the actual parent is absent or unsatisfactory.

## survivor guilt

A sense of guilt suffered by people who have survived a war, natural disaster, or other situation in which many other people died. It is characteristic of such guilt for sufferers to be constantly asking themselves both 'Why should I have lived when others died?' and 'Could I have done more to save others?'. Sometimes there is a real basis for this in that, given the instinctive desire for self-preservation, people often do think only of their own survival and can even forget the safety of their own children. In the particular case of Holocaust survivors, the continued guilt and mental suffering can be a sort of memorial to the dead, who would be betrayed if the survivors went on to live a normal life. Survivor guilt can be seen as a way of dealing with the feelings of helplessness experienced at the time of the situation: if one can blame oneself, then it gives more of a feeling of having been in control.

**symbiosis** /sɪmbɪˈousɪs/

Greek, 'the state of living together'. In biology the term refers to the relationship between two mutually dependent organisms of different species, but in psychology it is applied to close relationships between people living together in an interdependent way. The relationship between a mother and new-born infant is often given as an example of a symbiotic relationship. However, there is often a suggestion of a pathological element in symbiotic relationships: for example in **sado-masochistic** partnerships, in parent-child or husband-wife relationships where the mutual dependence is excessive, and in families where relationships depend on the members propping up each other's **neuroses**.

**symbol**

Anything that serves to represent, refer to, or signify something else; from Greek, 'sign, token'. *Symbolism* is making use of symbols. The terms are used in several ways in **psychoanalysis**, but always with the idea of a symbol as an **unconscious** disguise covering the true meaning of the thing represented. Symbols are particularly relevant to **dream analysis**, where it is accepted that repressed desires and thoughts express themselves symbolically in dreams. The term *universal symbol* is applied to symbols which tend to represent the same thing for virtually all people, and which occur in mythology and art as well as in dreams. An *individual symbol* is one whose meaning is specific to an individual.

See also **phallic symbol**

**sympathy**

The ability to feel with someone else; from Greek *sym-* 'together with' + *pathos* 'suffering, emotion'. The term strictly means sharing in the feelings of another person and undergoing the same emotions, but it is often popularly used as a synonym for **empathy** to mean feeling for people and understanding what they are undergoing. The real distinction between sympathy and empathy is that the former is more of an emotional experience and the latter more of an intellectual one.

## systematic desensitization
See **desensitization**

# T

## taboo

Anything that is banned or prohibited; from Polynesian *tabu*, referring to things that were set aside as sacred and therefore forbidden for use in any but a religious context. The term is used generally in psychology for social prohibitions on particular kinds of behaviour. In **psychoanalysis** it refers to prohibitions on deeply repressed sexual instincts that are socially unacceptable, particularly incestuous feelings.

## taboo on tenderness

A term invented by the Scottish psychiatrist Ian Suttie (1889–1935) to refer to the social prohibition on displays of emotion, vulnerability, and soft-heartedness. This applies particularly to boys who, as soon as they are out of infancy, are generally encouraged to be tough and 'manly' and discouraged from expressing their emotions and affections. They grow into intolerant, rigid adults who are embarrassed by demonstrations or discussions of the emotions, and shrink from anything that they interpret as 'sentimentality'. Since Suttie was writing, the taboo on tenderness has become less prevalent, partly through child psychologists encouraging mutual shows of affection between parents and children, and also because of the emphasis by the later feminist movement on the value of tender emotions for both sexes.

## TAT

See **Thematic Apperception Test**

## team counselling

See **co-counselling**

## telepathy

A form of **extrasensory perception** involving apparent communication from one person's mind to another's, without using any of the usual sensory channels; from Greek *tele* 'far off, from a distance' + *pathos* 'feeling'. Research studies on telepathy usually involve one person, the 'sender', looking at playing cards while the 'receiver' – separated from all possibility of communication with the sender – says what card is being looked at. Results of such research rarely show scores that are higher than one might expect by chance.

## tender-minded

A description of a personality type in the categorization of personalities devised by the American psychologist William James (1842–1910). The tender-minded person is idealistic, usually religious, and tends towards optimism. The concept has been extended by the German-born British psychologist H J Eysenck (1916– ), in his study of politics and personality, to apply to political **attitudes** that are associated with the traditional tender-mindedness traits but might be either radical (eg against war and harsh immigration laws) or conservative (eg against abortion and for compulsory religious education). See also **tough-minded**

## territoriality

The behaviour associated with marking out a piece of territory as belonging to oneself or one's group, and defending it. Originally this concept was applied only to animals, but it is also used in **social psychology** to describe human behaviour. It is common for both humans and animals to exhibit territorial behaviour in relation to their *primary territory* (usually the home in the case of humans), and to become uneasy or exhibit signs of **aggression** if they feel they are being 'invaded'. The space that is defended is not always an actual physical area, but might be a psychological one. See also **personal space**

## test anxiety

A term that means exactly what it says: **anxiety**, nervousness, and distress related to taking a test. When test anxiety is high, it is likely to affect an individual's performance, giving that person a lower score than expected.

## test sophistication

The amount of knowledge about, and experience of, psychological tests that a subject has. At the one extreme is the **naive**

**subject**, who knows nothing about the content or procedure of such tests and has no prior expectations. At the other is the *test-wise* person, who may have undergone a great many tests and be thoroughly familiar with the content of all the most common tests. Obviously the more test sophistication that people have, the higher they are likely to score on tests. When subjects actually have knowledge about the structure and analysis of a test, as well as its content, the results are likely to be very much distorted. On a **personality** test, for example, such subjects would be tempted to give the answers that they know will show their personality in the most advantageous light.

## t-group
See **sensitivity training**

## Thanatos
See **death instinct**

## Thematic Apperception Test (TAT)
One of the most commonly used **projective techniques**, developed by the American psychologist Henry A Murray (1893–1988) in the 1930s. The test involves showing the subject a series of 20 standard pictures, each one showing an ambiguous scene, usually involving one or more people. The subject is asked to tell a story about each picture, explaining what had happened prior to the scene, what was the present situation depicted, and what would happen in the future. The answers are analysed in terms of the themes that emerge, and are supposed to give insight into the subject's personality and motivations, and to reveal their emotional conflicts, needs, and fears.

## therapeutic community
A setting established for therapeutic purposes, in which patients live, and where every aspect of the environment has been designed to serve a function within the therapy. The term is not applicable to all institutions designed to treat psychological disturbances, but only to those where **milieu therapy** is practised, and where there is a strong belief that a controlled environment can aid treatment.

## thought stopping

A technique used in directive forms of **behaviour modification**, such as **rational emotive therapy**. Patients are asked to express their thoughts aloud, but when they say anything that indicates a thought or way of thinking that the therapy is intended to discourage, the therapist shouts 'Stop!'. The idea is that the patients will learn to do this for themselves, interrupting their thoughts whenever they are negative or counter-productive, and will eventually stop having such thoughts.

## threshold

A word used in various ways, usually in **experimental psychology**, where the primary meaning is the amount of a stimulus necessary in order to produce a perceptible effect. This is also known as the *absolute threshold*. The *differential threshold* is the point at which one can tell the difference between two different stimuli. The idea of threshold can occur in **psychoanalytic** theories, where it is assumed that tension and frustration have to go beyond a certain threshold in order to trigger off **anxiety** and **defence mechanisms**. Sometimes the word *limen* (the Latin equivalent) is used as a synonym for threshold, and also in words such as *subliminal*, 'below a threshold' and *supraliminal*, 'above a threshold'.

## token economy

A form of **behaviour modification** that operates in some institutions such as psychiatric hospitals, prisons and young offenders' institutes, or schools for children with **behaviour disorders**. Tokens (either points or physical objects like counters) are earned as a **reinforcement** for appropriate and desirable behaviour, and can then be cashed in for real rewards and/or privileges.

## tolerance of ambiguity

The ability to cope with situations that are ambiguous, ie capable of being interpreted in more than one way and not clear-cut. The person with a high tolerance of ambiguity is not made anxious by complex situations or relationships, and this is believed to be a trait indicating a mature **personality**. The opposite trait, *intolerance of ambiguity*, is marked by a strong preference for straightforward black-and-white situations and simplistic explanations.

## touch

See **in touch**

## tough-minded

A description of a personality type in William James's categorization (see **tender-minded**). The tough-minded person is materialistic, pragmatic, pessimistic, and usually irreligious. In Eysenck's study of the political implications of these traits, tough-minded people were shown to have racist views and to favour harsh penal laws, while also supporting liberal legislation on such issues as abortion, divorce, and Sunday trading.

## Tourette's syndrome

A disorder with neurological causes, named after the French psychiatrist Georges Gilles de la Tourette (1857–1904). In its mild form the only symptoms are involuntary facial tics and bodily movements. In more advanced cases these movements are exaggerated and accompanied by an uncontrollable need to make loud meaningless noises and to use obscene language.

## training analysis

The course of **psychoanalysis** that is undergone by those training to become **psychoanalysts**. All recognized institutes of psychoanalysis insist on such analysis – usually lasting five or six years – as an essential part of professional training. The analysis is as rigorous as that of therapeutic analysis of patients, as it is believed that potential psychoanalysts need to have a very thorough knowledge of their own **unconscious** and their own weaknesses in order to have insight into the unconscious of their patients and to withstand the emotional demands of analysing patients.

## trance

A state of reduced consciousness resembling sleep; from Latin *transire* 'to pass through, pass away'. The reference is to the passage into death, and most forms of trance are characterized by deep death-like sleep with reduced physical functioning. The trance that is induced in **hypnosis** is of this order: the subject generally appears to be in a deep sleep and to have surrendered control of his or her mind and will to the hypnotist. Trance states are also sometimes encountered in patients with psychiatric disorders, particularly those associated with **hysteria**. The word is also used for the state of deep absorption and dissociation from mundane matters shown by religious mystics and spiritualist mediums. However, people in these states do not in general experience the reduction in physical functioning usually associated with a trance.

## transactional analysis

A form of **group therapy** invented by the American psychologist Eric Berne (1910–70). The transactions – that is, the personal interrelations – between members of the group are analysed to reveal how members adopt parental, adult, or child roles in relation to each other. The primary aim of therapy is for clients to learn to control childish impulses and to reach a mature and realistic way of dealing with problems and relationships.

## transference

In **psychoanalysis**, the emotions of the patient towards the analyst; in particular the way in which patients transfer the **attitudes** and emotions associated with a particularly important person in their life – usually a parent – on to the analyst. This aspect of the analytic relationship is known as the *transference relationship*; when the patient's feelings towards the analyst are good, the relationship is one of *positive transference*, and when hostile it is one of *negative transference*. Transference is usually seen as a usual and even essential aspect of psychoanalytic treatment, of value in helping both patient and analyst better to understand the patient's emotions towards the parent or other person. The term is also used more generally, outside the context of psychoanalysis, to describe the way in which people transfer their feelings about one person on to another person.

See also **counter-transference**

## transsexualism

**Gender-identity disorder** in men and women who are biologically normal, characterized by the belief that they truly belong to the opposite sex and have been trapped into the wrong body. The feeling that their bodies – particularly their genitals – are inappropriate to them, is experienced by most transsexuals at a very early age. Many transsexuals seek what is popularly called a 'sex change operation' (officially known as *gender reassignment surgery*) combined with hormone treatment, and are then able to live the rest of their lives successfully as members of the opposite sex. The condition should not be confused with **homosexuality**. Not all transsexuals are homosexual, and their discomfort is directed at their bodies and the totality of the roles that are associated with their gender, not just the expected sexual role.

## transvestism

A **gender-identity disorder** characterized by the desire to dress in the clothes associated with the opposite sex in order to obtain sexual excitement. It is usually applied to men, probably because it is very common for women to wear trousers but much more unusual for men to wear skirts and dresses. Transvestites may or may not be **homosexual**; their condition is quite different from **transsexualism** in that transvestites are perfectly happy with their gender and have no desire to change it.

## trauma

Greek, 'wound'. In medicine it is applied to physical injuries and their physical effects, but in psychology and **psychiatry** it is applied to experiences that cause psychological damage and shock, and to the effects of such incidents. These experiences might actually be of physical injury, such as in *traumatic psychosis*, where an injury to the brain can cause a psychotic disorder. In *traumatic neurosis* the trauma can be a physical injury, a severe shock or fright, or a very unpleasant experience, after which a person displays symptoms of **neurosis**. **Amnesia** can also be caused by either physical or psychological trauma. In **psychoanalysis**, an *infantile trauma* is a shock or very disturbing experience that happened in infancy or early childhood, and which later causes a neurosis to develop.

See also **birth trauma; post-traumatic stress disorder**

## trial-and-error learning

In psychological theories of learning, the procedure by which the learner tries various methods of grasping material or solving a problem, gradually eliminating those that do not work. This was at one time thought to be the universal method by which complex learning operations take place, but it has since been realized that other methods are often used, including observation of others and **insight learning**.

See also **vicarious trial-and-error**

## twin studies

Studies carried out on pairs of twins in order to investigate the influence of heredity and environment on **intelligence**, behaviour, etc (see **nature-nurture controversy**). There has been particular interest in studying identical twins who have been brought up in different families. Such twins, of course, share identical genetic characteristics. If they have had different backgrounds, then similarities between the twins point to the influence of hereditary factors, while differences indicate the importance of environment. On the intelligence issue it has been found that while there are larger differences between identical twins who were reared apart than between such twins who were reared together, these differences are still not as great as those found in non-identical twins or ordinary siblings who were reared together.

## type A personality

A **personality** that is characterized by a strong desire for achievement and success, obsessive punctuality, a need to be in control, and an intolerance of inefficiency in others. The Type A person is always in a hurry and has neither time nor patience for self-reflection. This kind of personality is the opposite of the **type B personality**.

## type B personality

A **personality** that is marked by being relaxed and 'laid-back'. The Type B personality is unambitious, easy-going, and given to self-reflection. Although such a person is not likely to succeed as well in business as someone with a **type A personality**, he or she is probably in less danger of suffering from ulcers or having a heart attack. As with all 'type theories' of personality, most people do not fit into either of the two extremes described, although questionnaires have been designed to reveal where people's personalities lie in the continuum between types A and B.

# U

## unconditioned response

In **classical conditioning**, the naturally occurring response to a stimulus. This response is already present at the start of a conditioning experiment and does not have to be learned. In Pavlov's famous experiments, the unconditioned response was the dog's salivation when food was produced.

## unconditioned stimulus

See **classical conditioning**

## unconscious

Generally, in psychology, not being **conscious**, due to sleep, coma, fainting, or other physical causes. It also has the meaning, both as a noun and an adjective, of lack of, or lacking, awareness, particularly not being conscious of internal processes. This sense has more connection with the word's most significant use, within **psychoanalysis**, where it refers to the mental processes that people are not conscious of, and the area of the mind where such mental processes take place. In **Freudian** theory, the unconscious is the area where the repressed impulses of the **id** operate, that is, memories, desires and conflicts which are too disturbing for the conscious mind to deal with. The **inhibition** and **repression** of these impulses and memories lead to the development of **neurosis**. The unconscious must be distinguished from the **preconscious** and the **subconscious**, both terms that refer to processes which, while not conscious, are not repressed.

See also **collective unconscious**

## underachievement

Mainly in **educational psychology**, performance that is below the level which would be predicted. The basis of prediction is usually the score achieved on an **intelligence test**, but the 'underachiever' label is sometimes attached to children because their teachers have formed a general impression that they are brighter than their school performance indicates and are just 'not trying'.

See also **overachievement**

## undoing

In **psychoanalysis**, a **defence mechanism** by which people attempt to 'undo' something that they have said, thought, or done in the past, and have later regretted. Children, in particular, often attempt to cancel out past acts by a kind of magical ritual where they may mentally or physically re-enact the scene, while changing the actual piece of behaviour that they wish had never happened. It is thought that this ritualistic attempt to change the realities of the past is the mechanism operating in **obsessive-compulsive disorders**.

# V

### verbal tests

Any tests which centre on the subjects' abilities in verbal communication or language skills, as compared with **performance tests**. Verbal tests are sometimes actual tests of vocabulary knowledge. More often, however, the verbal content is less obvious, but the test is still ultimately dependent on the subject understanding the words used in the questions and being able to communicate an appropriate written or spoken response. Scores on verbal tests tend to remain fairly constant throughout adult life.

### vicarious trial-and-error (VTE)

*Vicarious* comes from Latin, 'substitution', putting something in the place of another. In vicarious trial-and-error, mental processes are substituted for physical ones. For example, in a chess game, a player may mentally rehearse moves before making an actual move. The term is often used in experiments involving animals learning their way through a maze, to describe the situation where the animal hesitates at a junction, as though it is thinking through the various possibilities.

### vocational counselling

**Counselling** focused on advising clients about their choice of occupation or career; also sometimes called **career counselling**. Vocational counselling is not used by employers attempting to find the right person for a job: it is a matter of discovering what skills, abilities, and aptitudes a person has, and trying to find the sort of work that would best fit these qualities. Vocational counselling has traditionally been used with young people about to leave school or higher education, but increasingly it is open to older people who are either voluntarily seeking a career change or have been forced to do so because of redundancy.

# W

## Wechsler Scales /ˈwɛkslər/

A general term for the **intelligence tests** devised by the American psychologist David Wechsler (1896–1981), and consisting of both **verbal test** and **performance test** elements. The Wechsler Adult Intelligence Scale (*WAIS*) is one of the most commonly used measures for testing adult intelligence. The verbal items include tests of vocabulary, comprehension, general knowledge, and arithmetic; the performance items include picture completion and spatial relations. The measure has been adapted for use with children and adolescents in the Wechsler Intelligence Scale for Children. This is usually abbreviated to *WISC*, and the post-1974 revised version is known as the *WISC-R*. There is also a Wechsler Preschool and Primary Scale of Intelligence (*WPPSI*) for use with children under 6. All these tests are designed to be administered to individuals rather than groups.

## wish-fulfilment

In **psychoanalysis**, the process by which the desires of the **id** are realized in the imagination, and tension caused by their non-fulfilment is therefore eased. Wish-fulfilment takes place primarily in dreams and in **fantasy**, also sometimes in neurotic symptoms and in the **Freudian slip**. Wish-fulfilment takes place in the **unconscious** and is not the same as *wishful thinking*, in which people consciously misjudge reality, telling themselves that what they wish is actually the case.

## withdrawal

A term used in several different ways in psychology. It can refer to a person removing him/herself from normal day-by-day living routines, gradually retreating from reality and becoming uncommunicative and uncooperative with others. This is a common symptom of **schizophrenia** and similar disorders, and the patient frequently seeks refuge from reality in alcohol or drug abuse. The term is also used for a thought-out strategic retreat from a particular situation, and for the behaviour exhibited by an animal that is losing a fight and wishes to withdraw from the scene without suffering further damage. In **psychiatry** and other areas where **drug therapy** is used, withdrawal applies to stopping the use of a drug, usually one on which a person has become dependent, and whose absence will cause *withdrawal symptoms*.

## word association test

A test of psychological reactions in which subjects are given a list of words to which they have to respond instantly. Repressed emotions are supposed to be revealed both by the responses and by the subjects' hesitations when confronting some words. These tests are also sometimes called *free association tests*, but there is little connection with the **psychoanalytic** meaning of **free association**, and the tests are not normally used by psychoanalysts or psychotherapists. Word association tests have been used by law enforcement agencies investigating criminal suspects. In these cases the tests are used in conjunction with **lie detectors** in order to test subjects' reactions to words that have a particular significance in relation to the crime being investigated. At one time these tests were also fashionable as a sort of parlour game for amateur psychologists.

## word salad

A jumble of apparently unconnected words and phrases characteristic of the speech of certain patients suffering from **aphasia** or **schizophrenia**. The 'salad' refers to the way in which the various disparate words and ideas are thrown together, failing to make any kind of coherent whole.

## working through

In **psychoanalysis**, and also in other forms of **psychotherapy**, the process by which patients gradually overcome their **resistance**, come to accept the implications of the therapist's interpretations, and gain insights into their problems. The term is also used in a looser way by some **psychotherapists** and counsellors to describe the process by which people come to terms with a painful situation, for example 'working through mourning' after bereavement.

# X

**xenophobia** /zɛnəˈfoʊbiə/

Fear of strangers or strange places, or fear of foreigners and anything foreign; from the Greek *xeno* 'stranger' + **phobia**. Fear of strangers or of being in a strange place is usually a genuine phobia, with the accompanying symptoms. However, the word is frequently used for an extreme dislike or distrust of foreigners, rather than a real phobia connected with them.